IN TOUCH

A selection by
Michael van Gessel
Antonio Angelillo
Lilli Lička
Tone Lindheim
João Ferreira Nunes

Edited by
LAE FOUNDATION
Lisa Diedrich
Mark Hendriks
Thierry Kandjee
Claudia Moll

BIRKHÄUSER BASEL
BLAUWDRUK WAGENINGEN

This is the third publication that the European Federation for Landscape Architecture is proud to be able to promote. *In Touch* follows *On Site* and *Fieldwork* as a celebration of some of the most outstanding landscape architectural designs, constructions and interventions across Europe.

As president of the Federation, I am regularly called upon to substantiate landscape architecture as a unique, stand-alone profession that demands its own educational input, standards and professional practice operations. There is no better way for promotion than via a publication such as this. You will find as you read through this book not only some of the best practice examples of implemented works of landscape architects across Europe but also some wonderful essays and discussions from a variety of eminent professionals we boast among our ranks of contemporary landscape architects.

Once again this work is a celebration of who we are and what we do. *In Touch* as a title could not be more pertinent. Landscapes in the twenty-first century remain all about people and the communities that have become established within them. Landscapes touch and reflect the culture, heritage, history, socio-economics and political interventions of the human population across the planet. They are a finite resource that we all need to respect and appreciate at a scale that has finally become prominent on most political agendas. It is up to us within the profession to ensure their importance and significance remain at the forefront of political discussions for the sustained future of life on the planet. Some may feel this is a gross exaggeration of our importance; I would remind them that we, as landscape architects, have the power and ability to shape the land, to create communities and to promote a landscape that can determine a sustainable future for everyone. No other profession can boast such credentials. Thus, it becomes ever more important that we stay *In Touch*.

Some may question the relevance and 'sustainability' of promotion of our work in written format with the suggestion that perhaps we, of all professions, should more readily embrace the digital, online format. This argument might hold true if our fellow built-environment professionals more readily accepted our profession around the world. Unfortunately, this is not the case. Thus, more tangible promotion of our work is called for. It is hoped that once again this book will enable those less enlightened in relation to our profession to appreciate better what it is we are capable of and how dependent a sustainable future of our planet is upon the appropriate engagement of trained landscape architects in all developmental aspects of the built environment.

I would like to finish by thanking everyone who has been involved in the making of this book; those submitting entries, the jury members, sponsors, publishers and editors alike – once again, well done.

Nigel Thorne

Nigel Thorne is a landscape architect, president of the European Federation for Landscape Architecture (EFLA) and vice-president of the International Federation of Landscape Architects (IFLA)

FOREWORD

With the passing of time LAE is gaining experience in the task of registering the state of the art in landscape architecture in Europe, and disseminating the information in a succession of books. Our ambition to improve our product keeps growing.

This is the third edition of the LAE book since 2002 and, when one looks at the content of the successive publications, a notable change is already apparent. The reader will notice that a new approach has been adopted in this book. More emphasis on reflection about the why and how is a definite improvement, and helps bring out the best of landscape architecture in Europe. In the meantime the production of a book as complex and complete as 'In Touch' is both an amazing and a heartening feat.

Amazing, because at a time when economies are at a low ebb and subsidies and sponsorships hard to come by, the financial basis for this undertaking that is so dependent on outside funding turned out to be (more or less) sufficient to start production. This is thanks to the efforts of a few dedicated people.

Heartening, because once again a number of highly motivated and qualified professionals were willing to devote much of their time and energy to adjudication and editorial responsibilities. Their names and qualifications are found in the imprint in the back of the book. They come and go over time because a new jury and editorial board are assembled for each edition. This edition profits from the work of the third jury and the third editorial board. The composition of the Board of the Foundation also changes: its founding members resigned in 2010 after eight years, and the second Board is now in place.

There is however a permanent core group on whom so much has depended: the chairman of the jury Michael van Gessel, editor-in-chief Lisa Diedrich, the producer of the book Harry Harsema, and editor Mark Hendriks. All have put in an enormous effort over the past ten years, and the success of the LAE series owes a great deal to their dedication. As parting chairman of the Board of the Foundation, I especially salute these 'pillars' of LAE for their unrelenting efforts.

Meto Vroom

Meto Vroom is professor emeritus of Landscape Architecture at Wageningen University, the Netherlands, and chairman of

REYKJAVIK

SELJORD

HERNING

ODENSE COPENHAGEN

TULLAMORE

FRIESLAND
DRENTHE
BERLIN
AMSTERDAM TWENTE
MAGDEBURG
CULEMBORG
ESSEN

LONDON

MUNICH VIENNA
WEIACH
SERMANGE ZURICH WINTERTHUR
BERN
LAUSANNE
LJUBLJANA
MARGHERA
BADALUCCO

BILBAO
CADAQUÉS
FIGUERAS
VILABLAREIX BEGUR
BARCELONA

LISBON

CONTENTS

CONTENTS

JOÃO FERREIRA NUNES JURY _

MICHAEL VAN GESSEL CHAIRMAN JURY _

LILLI LIČKA JURY _
TONE LINDHEIM JURY _

ANTONIO ANGELILLO JURY _

THIERRY KANDJEE EDITOR _

LISA DIEDRICH CHIEF EDITOR _

CLAUDIA MOLL EDITOR _
MARK HENDRIKS EDITOR _

HARRY HARSEMA PRODUCER _

THIERY KANDJEE EDITOR

LISA DIEDRICH CHIEF EDITOR

In Touch

Prologue by Lisa Diedrich

As an undertaking, Landscape Architecture Europe (LAE) has been observing and judging contemporary landscape architectural design practice for ten years now, throughout the first decade of the 21st century. *Fieldwork*, *On Site*, and the present third edition, *In Touch*, scrutinize works from 2001 to 2010. Within this decade, much has changed in the European 'landscape world', as it has in the world in general – the globalized world. We started the book series with the intention of communicating about the particular value of European landscape architecture, hence the title of the series. On the way, we came to realize that this claim is also a question: is there such a thing as European landscape architecture, and if so what binds it together, what are the shared values? Over the editions we found out that we have to take a deeper look, into and beyond the built projects.

Without a doubt, Europe features an outstanding body of landscape architectural work in quantitative terms, from which on each occasion our juries have selected a number of projects of outstanding design quality. Nearly all countries are represented too – except for the Eastern European countries where so far few works have met the juries' quality requirements. Perhaps this is because the landscape architectural profession there has only just started to shape itself through new independent practices, new university curricula, new planning authorities and different clients. Moreover, it does not share the same 20th century professional experience as the Western countries. So it might be that a particular political, economic and social context – synthesized into a professional discourse we could call our world of thought, the ethics and aesthetics of the profession, a kind of software – engenders designed and built work of quality, our hardware. If European landscape architecture builds on a common understanding and yet produces quality works of very different expression and style, then we should search not only for commonalities in the works but also in thought – and publish about both. The answer to our initial question of what binds our European design work together, we would venture, is: our thinking. Convictions, questions, intuitions, findings, experiences. If this is indeed the case, we shouldn't leave this European mindset under the surface of the water. Explore it. Get in touch.

This is the agenda of the third book, *In Touch*. Using our rigorous method of collecting, selecting and editing projects and discussions, we have concentrated this time on an in-depth analysis of the state of the art. As usual, we received roughly 500 entries in response to our call for submissions in late 2010. Our jury members studied them individually at home, then debated and selected together over two long weekends in early 2011 at the Schip van Blaauw, our 'factory' in the Dutch university town of Wageningen. During the first weekend the jury made an initial selection of around 50 projects, and then narrowed the choice down to 11 during the second weekend. We decided to look at a few projects in depth, and to present a greater number of projects in a very compact way. If we imagine a project as an iceberg, this book displays a wide panorama of icebergs – of which we admire the tips above the water surface – and a small expedition zone of bergs, of which we also explore the submarine depths. Consequently the 11 outstanding projects that we selected now form the main corpus of the book. They are generously presented as 'features' on many pages with a detailed project critique written by the LAE editors, and are richly illustrated. They are accompanied by essays by knowledgeable authors who discuss in depth the fundamental issues the feature projects address. The other selected projects constitute the critical mass of high-quality references, the 'icons'. They are grouped thematically and linked to one of the feature-essay ensembles. Each of them demonstrates an important aspect of contemporary practice, which is displayed through a short commentary by the jury on the project, and clear illustrations.

The limited number of main projects has allowed us to approach them differently than in the previous two editions. This time the LAE editors visited their projects, and talked to designers and clients on site. Instead of anonymous, seemingly neutral, project descriptions, they have written signed project critiques, expressing their positions, and they have set up their investigations according to the Drawing and Reading methodology defined by Danish landscape architect and scholar Malene Hauxner. Having been a practitioner herself before moving into academia, she strove to overcome the common reduction of design work to mysterious arty stuff that could only be judged by taste and instead established a framework for a qualitative analysis that helps towards making well-founded judgments of landscape architectural design. She provided an academic method for the evaluation of artistic work, approaching the work from two opposing points of view: the scientific-structuralist one, inherited from modernism, which would cast light upon the morphology and the syntax of a work, its facts and forms, almost as if detached from the surroundings, and the interpretative-semiotic one, inspired by postmodernism, which would investigate the various facets of the work's context, its exegesis, the understanding of its broader cultural milieu, its innumerable relationships and meanings, subjectively scrutinized without pretending to find universal truth but offering a qualified guess: 'abduction' in her words. Our project critiques are not intended to be academic texts. Rather, they rely on our wish to make well-grounded judgments of design works in the journalistic genre of a project critique, and we continue to refine our skills. By doing so, tacit criteria will become explicit; disciplinary thinking will become apparent. And these are some of the explorations the profession needs: getting in touch with the things below the surface of the water.

Malene Hauxner was one of the best brains of this enterprise and we mourn her passing – she left us this year, far too soon. She was among our first essay authors and qualified late-20th-century European landscape architectural design tendencies as 'either/or, less and more' in our first book *Fieldwork*. Hauxner was a theoretician of practice, aiming at providing design work with an adequate treatment in academia. Our objective is to feed her academic findings back into practice – close to her spirit, we are practitioners of thought.

During the jury weekends, we discussed issues that, while not explicitly addressed by the designers, seemed to have deeply influenced their design choices or their ways of designing. Research is one of these issues, more specifically: research on, for and by design. So far it is mostly prevalent overseas, in the Anglo-Saxon world; continental Europe is only slowly starting to embrace it. Here and there offices devote time to methodical research as an important part of their design work, and a few academics have made design procedures an integral component of their research. The jury, however, had its doubts about the quality of the submitted projects of this kind. They selected one 'icon', Wadden Coast Landscape Vision, and handed the issue, which shows much promise, over to the editors, who decided to invite

MICHAEL VAN GESSEL, born in 1948, trained as a landscape architect at the University of Wageningen where he graduated in 1978. He is now active in the broader field of landscape architecture and urbanism, having worked since 1997 as an independent advisor. Prior to this he was employed for 18 years at Bureau B+B (urbanism and landscape architecture), the last seven as its director. He devotes half his time to the supervision of large-scale projects, which have included the Belvédère development in Maastricht and the redevelopment of the IJ South Bank (a former harbour area) in Amsterdam. Landscape architectural projects take up the rest of his time. For each project he selects the people best suited for the work at hand – an effective networking practice. Two monographs about his work have been published: *Michael van Gessel - Invisible Work* (2008) and *Michael van Gessel* (2011).
www.michaelvangessel.com

TONE LINDHEIM JURY

ANTONIO ANGELILLO JURY

TONE LINDHEIM, born in 1954, is a Norwegian landscape architect. After working on urban renewal projects for the City of Oslo, she and Jostein Bjørbekk set up Bjørbekk & Lindheim AS in 1986. She has been a professor of landscape architecture at the Norwegian University of Life Sciences since 1996. As a practising landscape architect, she focuses on directing large urban transformation projects, urban parks and spaces, housing areas and school grounds. Best known among these projects is the Nansen Park, the former airport that was redeveloped as a major recreational area. Tone Lindheim has been the chairman of the Norwegian Housing and City Planning Association, and has served on many competition juries. She is the author of *The good Back Yard* (1987), *The New Oslo* (1987), *Noise baffles in Oslo* (1995) and *School yards in Oslo* (1999). www.blark.no

ANTONIO ANGELILLO, born in 1961, graduated in 1986 from the IUAV University of Venice with a degree in architecture and now lives and works in Milan. After an internship period with Alvaro Siza in Porto he achieved success in numerous international architectural competitions. From 1989 to 1997 he was editor of *Casabella*, publishing articles on architecture and the modern metropolis. In 1994 he founded ACMA, the Italian Centre for Architecture, of which he is now the director. With ACMA he has worked extensively in Italy and abroad organizing exhibitions, seminars, meetings, workshops and competitio to promote sound urban planning and architecture. Since 1986 he has been a research fellow and lectur at several Italian universities. In 2008 he became t co-director of the Master c Landscape Architecture at the Polytechnic University Catalonia (UPC). www.acmaweb.com

a pioneer in the field to contribute with a richly illustrated 'feature essay' on creative knowledge. To be continued...

Nature was another issue that dominated the designers' project explanations and therefore also the jury's debate. The deconstruction of a 1960s holiday village on the Catalan coast earned special attention because of the Catalan government's forceful decision to demolish this much-praised architectural ensemble in order to re-establish 'nature', and also because of the way the designers have construed and constructed 'nature'. It would have been impossible to understand this mindset without looking into Catalan history, and we have therefore included an essay on the emergence of the Catalonian profession, with a long side-glance at the role of yet another outstanding soul of European landscape architecture whom we sorely miss: Bet Figueras, landscape architect in Barcelona and member of the LAE board died, far too soon, in early 2010. Her spirit is reflected in her built oeuvre, of which the jury selected two 'icons', through the lessons she taught to the next generation of Catalan designers, and through the lasting bonds she created between Barcelona and Europe, not least by her presence in the LAE Foundation – a true female chevalier de la profession. A discipline depends on the founding fathers and mothers who have shaped its thinking. We therefore continue our explorations on European pioneers, started in *Fieldwork*, with two other (hi)stories in addition to the Catalan contribution, namely on Swiss landscape architecture, which is not so Swiss at all, and on the Danish profession, which includes Swedish sources.

Yet a discipline profiles itself at least to the same extent by introducing new discourses and establishing the vocabulary required to express new figures of thought. Key questions that emerged from the jury's debates have therefore been included in the essays, which attempt to tackle subjects of high topical relevance. Besides nature and its relationship to artistic practice, we find it important to create deeper insight into the motives of landscape architectural language, into the question of how to design with history and heritage, and finally into the broad field of designing what we once called a European city and which is desperately in need of new names, discussions and designs. All essays dive deeper below the surface and in a different way than the 'features' do: they gather elements of a common European discourse in the making.

This book has faces and brains: it consists of people. Above all the jurors who spent long hours together before arriving at their choices, as the photos of the jury sessions depicted here show. For each LAE edition we provide the jury with a method of selection and the common discussion, but we do not give them a catalogue of predefined selection criteria. They prefer to develop their own framework of judgment while adjudicating, in hermeneutical circles of reflection, for every LAE edition anew. As in previous jury meetings, Dutch chairman Michael van Gessel felt the bonds that immediately grew between the jury members, even coming from different cultural backgrounds. There was an immediate understanding of each other's analyses, and little heated debate about the quality of a project in general. The tough and lengthy discussions took place around the thin line that separates good professional practice from real quality work, van Gessel reported, and this was confirmed by Norwegian Tone Lindheim, Austrian Lilli Lička, Italian Antonio Angelillo, and Portuguese João Nunes. In their eyes, the jury was looking especially for a designer's sense and sensitivity – arguing in favour of those designers bringing about projects that make sense, and that are sensual. The jury praised a designer's sense of withholding, his or her act of intervening only if necessary, with subtlety and elegance, while creating poetry from an in-between of what is suggested and what is actually made.

Michael van Gessel calls site-specific those solutions that ground a design intervention, fit it into a context, in harmony with nature and the environment, while making the work speak without shouting, and while executing it well. In his words: landscape architecture pur sang. According to Angelillo, there are also those projects that convinced the jury because of their quality of novel artistic practice and design research into unconventional situations, such as interstitial spaces and urban leftovers, oscillating in between public and private realms, inside and outside, open or closed. Lička recognizes design quality from the coherence between form, material, idea and site. Lindheim values projects that have an innovative and progressive content; if they are original and at the same time appealing to both heart and mind, or, in Nunes' words, characterized by extraordinary sensitivity, intelligence, wisdom and innovation. Furthermore, Nunes points out the quality that can be achieved by including a deep understanding of landscape processes in a design proposal. Angelillo's choice is discerning, appreciating only those projects that go beyond decorative stage setting, that propose solid structures which improve people's life in the urban realm, without, as Lindheim puts it, pompous design. Angelillo rates those projects that revive landscape architectural language by translating traditional tasks, like park or square design, into contemporary speech. All jurors agree that the future of the profession lies in intensifying and transforming what already exists, whether small scale or big scale. The challenge however, as Nunes points out, is that the humility and discretion of the landscape architectural profession might need a different momentum in order to face the avalanche of other professions claiming to cope better with transforming landscapes, public space, green rooms, parks, gardens, large-scale terrains... Lička calls for landscape architecture to become an even more relational practice, for example by becoming involved in regional planning for the outcome of a small park, by looking at materials from a globalized market perspective but in interaction with a neighbourhood – in a nutshell: designing across all geographical scales and including a range of societal issues.

This introduction explains our method and invites the reader to dive into the main part of the book, into the ocean of icebergs, with their heights and depths. We chose to end this edition with a critical evaluation of our enterprise. For this we asked Dutch emeritus professor of landscape architecture Meto Vroom, founding father and chairman of the LAE board, who is handing over his role to Michael van Gessel, to look back on a decade of landscape architectural design work and discourse as published in the pages of the books we have produced so far. He did more: he relates what he observes today to his experience spanning sixty years of professional involvement. His comprehensive essay traces some lines from current design work back to claims made and questions posed in the 20th century. Many of his questions merit further research, which we hope to develop with the help of designers and design researchers in new formats and in forthcoming editions.

So doing, we aim to set standards both in design and in design critique, animating disciplinary and interdisciplinary debate, creating theoretical knowledge that feeds back into landscape architectural practice. With every edition, our European network of professionals grows, and the members of the board, the jurors, the editors, and the essay authors are nourishing our enterprise, joining us and taking common thoughts back home. In this respect LAE is more than a book, it is a European commitment to an intense and personal way of moving the profession forward.

References
[1] Malene Hauxner, Drawing and Reading – a course script for teaching theory and method of landscape architecture at the University of Copenhagen, 2010

Lisa Diedrich is editor-in-chief of the Landscape Architecture Europe series and professor of landscape

JOÃO FERRREIRA NUNES, born in 1960, graduated in landscape architecture at the School of Agronomy at the Technical University of Lisbon in 1985 and obtained his master's degree in landscape architecture at the Polytechnic University of Barcelona (UPC) in 1996. In 1989 he founded the PROAP landscape architecture studio, building a large cross-disciplinary team of distinguished professionals. Today João Nunes is PROAP's international director, heading the three offices in Lisbon (Portugal), Luanda (Angola) and Treviso (Italy). He develops PROAP's conceptual and creative design and defines the strategic orientation of its research processes. In 1992 he was appointed professor at the School of Agronomy at the Technical University of Lisbon. He also lectures at various Italian universities.
www.proap.pt

LILLI LIČKA, born in 1963, studied landscape ecology and landscape architecture at the University of Natural Resources and Life Sciences (BOKU) in Vienna. In 1989 she was awarded a research grant to study the structure of urban open spaces in the Netherlands. After working for a year with B+B in Amsterdam she returned in 1991 to Vienna, where she started working on urban renewal projects in the city. This was when she founded koselička landscape architecture, together with her partner Ursula Kose. koselička carried out studies on public spaces and designed urban open spaces for open uses. In 2003 Lilli Lička was appointed professor of landscape architecture at Vienna's University for Natural Resources and Life Sciences (BOKU). She was president of the Austrian Federation of Landscape Architecture from 2004 to 2010 and is a member of the board for urban development and design at the City of Vienna.
www.koselicka.at

_LISA DIEDRICH CHIEF EDITOR

_TONE LINDHEIM JURY

_CLAUDIA MOLL EDITOR

LISA DIEDRICH, born 1965 in Minden (Germany), studied architecture and urbanism in Paris, Marseille and Stuttgart and science journalism in Berlin, becoming a specialist in contemporary European landscape architecture. From 1993 to 2000 she was one of the editors of *Topos European Landscape Magazine*. From 2000 to 2006 she worked as a consultant to Munich's chief architect at the city's public construction department. Since 2006 she has run her own consultancy in Munich, working among others as editor-in-chief of the book series *Landscape Architecture Europe (Fieldwork/ On Site/In Touch)* and of *'scape* the international magazine for landscape architecture and urbanism. In 2007 she returned to academia, and is currently a PhD fellow at the Centre for Forest and Landscape, University of Copenhagen. In 2012 she was appointed professor of landscape architecture at the Swedish University of Agricultural Sciences (SLU) in Alnarp/Malmö.

DAPHNE DE BRUIJN, born 1975 in Ede (the Netherlands), studied graphic design at Utrecht School of the Arts. She works for Blauwdruk Publishers on books and magazines in the field of landscape, urbanism and design. She has been the designer of the *Landscape Architecture Europe* series since its inception.

HARRY HARSEMA, born 1957 in Goor (the Netherlands), studied landscape architecture at Wageningen University and graduated in 1985. Since then he has worked as a journalist, editor and graphic designer in the field of landscape and architecture. He was founder, editor-in-chief and is now publisher of the Dutch magazine *Blauwe Kamer* and the Dutch *Yearbook for landscape architecture and urban design*, and is editor-in-chief of *'scape* magazine. In 1994 he founded Blauwdruk Publishers, which specializes in books on landscape architecture. He has been the producer of the *Landscape Architecture Europe* series since its inception.

MARK HENDRIKS, born 1980 in Tilburg (the Netherlands), studied spatial planning at Wageningen University. Since graduating in 2004 he has worked as a journalist, editor and author, covering spatial planning, urban planning and landscape architecture. He has worked on numerous publications in the field of urban and rural planning. He is an editor of the Dutch magazine *Blauwe Kamer* and is a regular contributor to the international *'scape* magazine. Since 2008 he has been a guest lecturer at the Academy of Architecture in Amsterdam and the Technical University Delft. He has been a member of the editorial board of the *Landscape Architecture Europe* series since its inception.

THIERRY KANDJEE, born 1973 in Tananarive (Madagascar), graduated as a landscape architect from the Ecole Nationale Supérieure du Paysage (ENSP) Versailles in 1999. He established TAKTYK [landscape + urbanism] in 2005 with the architect Sebastien Penfornis. With offices in Paris and Brussels, TAKTYK won the French Ministry of Culture award for young landscape architects in 2006, and the young urbanists prizes awarded by the French ministry of Ecology, Transport and Housing in 2010. In 2012 Taktyk has been awarded the Topos Landscape Award. Kandjee is a design studio lecturer at ENSP Versailles and French landscape state adviser. He also works on a practice based PhD with RMIT Melbourne.

CLAUDIA MOLL, born 1972 in Zurich (Switzerland), studied landscape architecture at the Hochschule für Technik Rapperswil and completed her postgraduate studies in history and theory of architecture at the Swiss Federal Institute of Technology, ETH Zurich. She has worked since 1994 in various Swiss landscape architecture offices and, from 2002 to 2003 she was editor of *Garten + Landschaft* and *Topos European Landscape Magazine* in Munich. Since 2004 she has been a scientific researcher at the Institute of Landscape Architecture, ETH Zurich, as well as a freelance journalist. In 2009 she and Axel Simon published the book *Eduard Neuenschwander. Architekt und Umweltgestalter.* Since 2011 she has been PhD fellow at the Institute of Landscape Architecture, ETH Zurich.

HARRY HARSEMA PRODUCER

MICHAEL VAN DE GESSEL CHAIRMAN JURY_

GROUNDS AND FRAMES

HERNING
COPENHAGEN

AMSTERDAM

ZURICH

LJUBLJANA

BADALUCCO

On a typical afternoon in the Funenpark children play freely between the buildings.

FUNENPARK

designed by LANDLAB studio voor landschapsarchitectuur

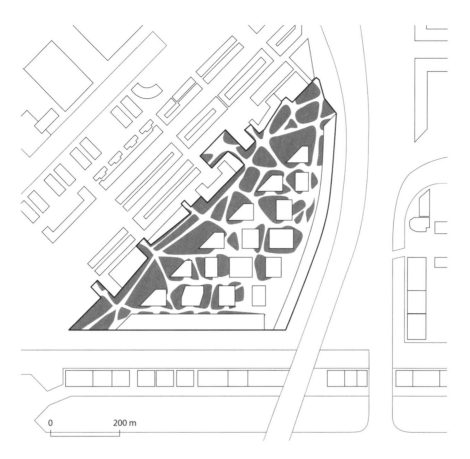

0   200 m

JURY COMMENT In contrast to the 'over-designed' projects being realized in many European cities, the concept behind Funenpark is simplicity itself. This gives it coherence and strength: the two types of paving stone in three shades occupy the outdoor space in a convincing manner. The result is a marvellous, campus-like environment that welds together the divergent architecture of the apartment buildings.

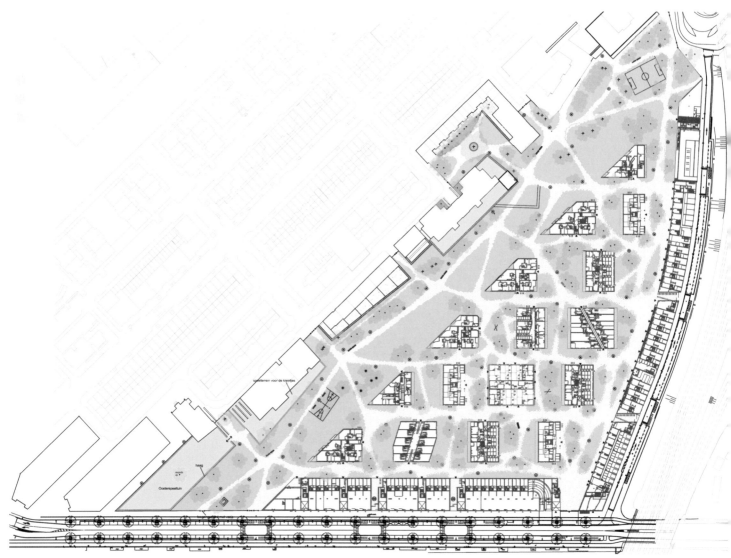

Ground plan.

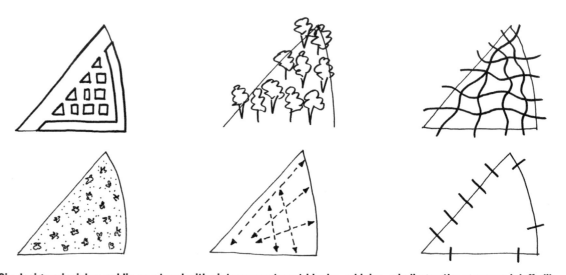

Six design principles: public courtyard with sixteen apartment blocks, robinias, winding paths, grass and daffodils, long view lines and connections with the surroundings.

From tiles to urban floor to floating space

Feature by Mark Hendriks

An outdoor space with the ambiance of an open field, where residents and passers-by wander freely through the space. This concept would seem to be incompatible with modern apartment complexes built in the heart of a big, busy city. But the Funenpark in Amsterdam proves that the opposite is true. Here, the space around sixteen newly built apartment blocks – with a density of 150 dwellings per hectare – has been designed as a modern variation on the traditional courtyard: as an open, informal area of parkland. The project echoes the traditions of seventeenth- and eighteenth-century Amsterdam, where densely built housing alternates with tranquil green courtyards.

The Funenpark is located on a former railway marshalling yard to the east of Amsterdam's city centre. The terrain is triangular in shape, bordered on the east by the railway to Utrecht, on the south by the Nieuwe Vaart canal and on the west by the narrow streets and the old workers' houses of the nineteenth-century Czar Peter neighbourhood. A newly constructed L-shaped residential and office building divides the Funenpark along its east and south sides from the surrounding area. The inner space is reached from the street via gateways (for bikes and pedestrians). The sixteen apartment buildings are arranged in rows. The paths that wind between the blocks are striking: the design drawing shows a trail in a 'fishnet stocking' design, which broadens out in a westerly direction. The paving consists simply of two different pentagonal concrete paving stones in three shades of grey, designed and made specially for Funenpark. The 21-cm-thick stones have been laid in a random fashion, resulting in a directionless and 'wild' mosaic. The paving pattern means that pedestrians and cyclists are not guided in a particular direction and are thus compelled to find their own way in a in a wandering fashion.

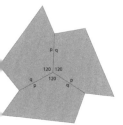  

e shape of the two 'Funen tiles' is the result of a mathematical exercise.

The shape of the two 'Funen tiles' is the result of an exhaustive mathematical exercise. The first step was to design the first five-sided tile with two equal, contiguous sides, at an angle of 120 degrees. Three of these tiles were then laid with the equal sides abutting each other – forming a 'windmill'. When the angle of the furthest corner of each separate tile is 60 degrees, it turns out that six 'windmills' fit together and form a circular 'flower' pattern. By cutting the hexagon that is formed in the middle of this 'flower' on the diagonal, the form and dimensions of the second 'Funen tile' emerge. The wild pattern is created by laying the paving stones in a random fashion.

The planting is modest: the mesh of the 'fishnet stocking' is grass with the odd daffodil. 170 Robinia trees have been planted throughout the park, their light crowns contrasting with the brick and glass facades of the apartment complexes. Between the sixteen residential blocks and the old Czar Peter neighbourhood, where the fishnet pathway 'widens out', lies an oblong shaped zone of open park space. A cycle path crosses the park, linking the Cruquiuskade in the south with the park entrance in the north. A piece of art will be placed in the middle, on the site of a former bastion. On the one hand the park zone forms a transition between the contemporary upbeat atmosphere of the Funenpark and the closed, brick social housing in the Czar Peter neighbourhood. On the other hand the park connects: the rear side of the workers' houses has now become the front side of the park. This has led to a number of measures: from gateways built in the wooden fencing to benches being placed. At one location the paving pattern and the grass from the Funenpark penetrate the nineteenth-century neighbourhood. A half-open courtyard with a plane tree has been transformed from a forgotten space into a pleasant meeting place.

The Funenpark narrowly escaped being landscaped like so many Dutch residential neighbourhoods: with the usual streets, pavements, parking spaces, and front and back gardens. But early on in the process doubts were expressed by the municipality of Amsterdam as to whether this was the right way to go about landscaping a new urban quarter in a location that was officially part of the old city centre: the area actually lies within the now-vanished ramparts of old Amsterdam. Landscape architect Bram Breedveld (LANDLAB) was asked to create a new design for the outside area. The designers came up with the idea of a luxuriant courtyard, an orderly outdoor space that forges unity between the sixteen apartment blocks without lapsing into a standard design of pavements and gardens. In order to create as large an open space as possible, the parking area has been built underground and private gardens have been omitted. The binding character of the outdoor space has benefited from simplicity: grass, robinias and just two types of paving stone in three shades.

The concept also had consequences for the architecture of the sixteen apartment blocks. The buildings had to be 'all round', because residents and visitors pass by all sides of the buildings as they walk along the winding paths. This has led to various solutions. Some facades are open and transparent, where use has been made of glass windows and sliding doors. Other buildings have a stone plinth, lending anonymity. In several places – especially along the L-shaped apartment building – the absence of gardens has resulted in informal initiatives, such as the introduction of plant pots, playground equipment and bicycle sheds. This fits well with the slightly anarchic character of a city like Amsterdam. On a typical afternoon in the Funenpark visitors and residents move freely between the buildings, reaching their destination in an intuitive manner – whether it be the entrance to their apartment block, the street or the Czar Peter neighbourhood. At city scale, the Funenpark is a 'hidden' stepping stone in the connection between the centre of Amsterdam, the eastern harbour area and IJburg, a new neighbourhood.

By LANDLAB studio voor landschapsarchitectuur (Bram Breedveld) In collaboration with O.S.L.O. (Martien van Osch) Programme Park design of a high density housing area Commissioned by City of Amsterdam, Heijmans property developers Area 4 ha Design 1999–2010 Implementation 2011 Budget € 2,300,000

park zone.

w of the entrance from the Czar Peter neighbourhood.

The paths wind between the blocks. Photo Jeroen Musch

View along the L-shaped building on the east side.
Photo Anne ten Ham

The design of the Funenpark invites informal use.

...nenpark fits well with the slightly anarchic character of a city like Amsterdam.

The mesh of the 'fishnet stocking' is grass. Photo Jeroen Musch

Essay by Steven Delva

WHY WE SHAPE SPACE

The landscape architect's task is to imbue the redesign of urban public space with meaning and potential for experiencing it. This is why we shape space, why we lend form to the grounds we walk on and to the elements that frame us. In this undertaking it is important that it is impossible to distinguish the old from the new, but that together they form a new and extraordinary entity. The landscape architect takes the context and individuality of a location as starting point, includes in the time factor and adopts an attitude of reticence. If the systematics of nature form part of the design, the landscape architect can venture further than the usual.

In contrast to architects, urban planners and other designers, landscape architects bear the responsibility of creating interesting spatial configurations that are shaped by factors that bring about change: the seasons, weather conditions, skies, plant cycles, soil conditions and time. Together these constitute the quintessential aspects of landscape architecture: it's about making use of dynamic, living processes instead of static, immutable situations. A good understanding of nature and how it works forms the foundation for diverging from the usual…. Thus tension arises between architecture, landscape, nature, art, ecology and culture. Even if, from a morphological point of view, design interventions such as *Funenpark*, the *Tivoli underpass*, the *HEART Museum*, the *Courtyard in Classengade* and the other examples in this section feature simple solutions for shaping just a horizontal ground plan or a vertical frame of urban space, landscape architecture is not simply about finding static forms for grounds and frames. Rather it is about composing these elements in constant motion and in relationship with their surroundings.

A powerful start can be made to the design process by daring to consider the site itself and its contextual stratification. What is the history of an area? Is there social cohesion? What economic activities take place there? It is important that all these aspects are included and valuable features that are present are used, so that existing qualities are given a new meaning. An urban space is never a blank page. Every site has its own distinctive history and unique story. This also determines how subtly and sustainably the space can be dealt with. It is up to the landscape architect to create the right conditions so that a process unfolds 'spontaneously'. In fact, everything is already there, and the existing public space is taken up, processed and put back again in a sublime way by the landscape architect. This means that newly shaped public spaces do not exist in isolation from their surroundings. A fine example of a subtle intervention is the *Tivoli underpass* at the Moderna Gallery in Ljubljana in Slovenia. In the new design the only addition is the cladding of the concrete walls, using an ingeniously shaped metal mesh, which protects against graffiti and produces an optical effect while walking past it. It is a design intervention that does not react against the present users, such as the homeless, and which also welcomes new users.

During the analytical and inventory phase there must be room for the designer's personal intuition. In fact this is essential: it is through the relationship between the historical vocabulary of what is present and the current attitude of the designer that the character of the space is determined, the result of the symbiosis between analytical data and artistic design. After detailed analysis – involving superimposing topographi-cal maps, aerial photos and ground plans – the investigative design work begins: a creative process in which emotion and intuition play an important role. Intuitive design is translated into an artistic and emotionally based search for the correct spatial effect: Which forms and contrasts do you apply? What proportions will create a pleasant space? What is the best location for functions or elements?

Design ambition goes together with modesty, unpretentious-ness. It's not about the designer's ego, but about the location itself. This must be 'listened' to, as only then does an under-standing arise of how the location can assume its form and function in its own way. The less intervention, the greater the effect. Landscape architects should not allow themselves to be influenced by non-sustainable relics from the present de-sign of public space. The designer's starting point should be a basic plan of the area, pared down to the bare essentials. A strong public space is formed by bringing about as powerful an experience as possible with as little variety as possible. This has been achieved with success in the design of the external space of the new *HEART Museum of Contemporary Art* in Hern-ing, Denmark. The feeling of space is maintained: a flagstone surface blends seamlessly with the surrounding landscape; the building, the square and the landscape form one entity. Another example is the *Funenpark* in Amsterdam. The effect of space has been achieved in a relatively small area of residen-tial blocks. This has been done by designing the space around the blocks in a sober and uniform way. It is the simplicity of the public space that is its strength and determines its form – which at first appears to be calm and reserved, but on second glance reveals fantastic detail. The ornamental detailing of a design – seating, lighting, kerbs and the smallest indication of a terrace area – is not prominent, but rather provides a coun-terweight to the clear and powerful main lines already there, and is intended to strengthen these. Well-thought out ornamental details contribute to the aesthetics as a whole, and are applied in an unobtrusive and refined manner. The effect on the visitor, user or passer by is to create a sensation of calm, beauty and lucidity. A well-known risk is that public spaces are easily deemed to be too bare. People prefer places to be more convivial. While one carefully chosen element in an otherwise empty space creates beauty and the aesthetic. Take the *Courtyard in Classengade*, a street in Copenhagen: the fountain in the centre is accentuated by the large-scale paving, which has been laid in a well-thought-out pattern. The proportions are right and the repetition of elements results in beauty: identical elements in a particular composition, which together form a new entity.

Public space that works should be pleasant for a small number of people, but at the same time must be able to accommodate larger numbers. Seating should not be an afterthought, but should be included during the design process. One way of creating places to sit, for example, is to deliberately raise a piece of lawn, or by a large-scale staircase. These make a public space an inviting place to spend time, and prevent them from becoming desolate even if a person is alone in the space. Plans and designs do not come to an end upon execution. A design must include conditions to ensure that it will continue to evolve throughout the course of its lifetime. The design should be regarded as an analytical yet intuitive link in time, where only the outlines are fixed. Every generation has the right to attach new value to urban spaces and to use them as they see fit. Likewise, it is their duty to maintain them well for the next generation.

Steven Delva is a Belgian landscape architect who set up DELVA Landscape Architects in 2009, with headquarters in Amsterdam and a subsidiary office in Antwerp.

A lacy twist turns the simple fence of the enclosed Lace Garden into a spatial delight. Photo Jeroen Musch

Consistent, poetic and quite simply beautiful: the enclosed Lace Garden in the courtyard of a social housing block in Amsterdam-West is a strong design. New trees were added to the existing ones, and between them single white-flowered plants, shrubs and bulbs were planted – all of which create the impression of a piece of lace when viewed from the houses. On three sides the garden is separated from the private gardens by beech hedges. On the fourth side a public green space borders the Lace Garden, set apart by a standard white wire mesh that is actually not so standard at all. Close inspection reveals an integrated lacy twist, turning the simple fence into an elegant spatial delight. It is more curtain than fence, its physical fragility rendering it more immaterial than material. Its allusions to refined feminine dresses transform the earthiness of the garden into a world of light dreams. [mh]

Programme Enclosed garden within the courtyard of a social housing block **Designer** Anouk Vogel **In collaboration with** Demakersvan (fence) **Commissioned by** Ymere **Area** 0.218 ha **Design** 2008–2009 **Implementation** 2010 **Budget** € 60,000

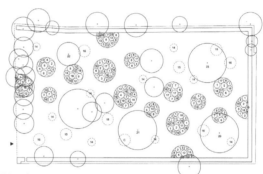

Planting plan.

Only single white-flowered plants and shrubs were planted.

MATTEOTTI SQUARE

designed by mag.MA architetture

A long grey bench rises out of the ground, balanced by sunken gravel borders.

A subtle geometric game is an apt description of the redesigned former car park in the town of Badalucco in northern Italy. The narrow, rectangular Matteotti square is surrounded by colourful houses. The pattern of shadows made by the high house fronts has been used to introduce seams in the rust-brown asphalt – inspired by the 'craquelure' mosaic that forms as dried mud or ceramics crack. Perpendicular to the seams in this two-dimensional design, a long grey bench rises out of the ground, balanced by sunken gravel borders in which native olive trees have been planted. Despite a limited budget, an original square has been made with the help of modest design interventions and clever use of materials – bitumen, reinforced cement, natural iron and mixed gravel were used for the hard surfacing of the square and the bench – that blend in with the Mediterranean atmosphere of the surrounding area. [mh]

Programme Design of a small urban square **Designer** mag.MA architetture **Commissioned by** Municipality of Badalucco **Area** 650 m² **Design** 2006–2007 **Implementation** 2007–2008 **Budget** € 112,500

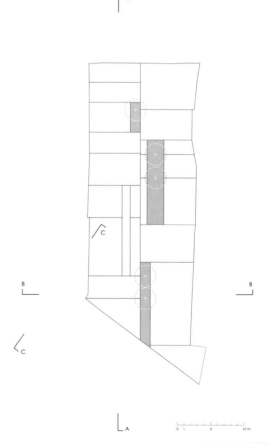

Ground plan.

The elegant and delicate 'rug' of bricks. Photo Anders Sune Berg

From the kitchen window, the pattern of the paving in the courtyard of a social housing complex in the Østerbro district of Copenhagen looks like a rug. The design, which uses yellow and grey bricks, is inspired by the ornaments and carvings that decorate the facades of buildings in the area. The intervention can almost be described as artistic even though it only involves a two-dimensional surface. Nevertheless, the design – its scale and in combination with the high yellow walls – has transformed the previously bleak asphalted courtyard into a place of character with a pleasing ambiance. Residents are still free to use the space as they wish: to park their bikes or adorn it with flowerpots and picnic tables. The elegant and delicate 'brick rug' – with an appealing fountain in its centre – ensures that the courtyard is used with respect and that the place doesn't degenerate into a junkyard. [mh]

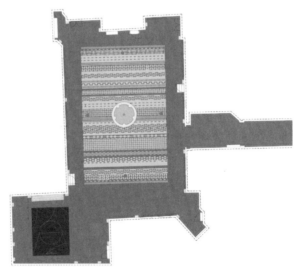

Design drawing.

Programme Renovation of a courtyard **Designer** 1:1 Landskab **Commissioned by** AB Store Classenhus **Area** 400 m² **Design** 2009–2010 **Implementation** 2010 **Budget** € 200,000

COURTYARD IN CLASSENGADE

designed by 1:1 Landskab

HEART'S OPEN SPACES

designed by Schønherr

The random flagstone pattern contrasts with the straight lines of the museum walls. Photo Roland Halbe

The architecture of the Herning Museum of Contemporary Art (HEART), designed by Steven Holl Architects, and its surrounding landscape are intimately connected. On the one hand, each is an extension of the other: the design of the outdoor space – which incorporates different forms and free compositions – is in tune with the elegant design of the museum's dish-shaped roof surface. The landscape around the building echoes this with its loosely designed water features, grassed areas and earthen embankments. On the other hand, the building and its surroundings contrast with each other. The random pattern of the loose flagstones in the main square stands in stark contrast to the severe concrete walls and large windows. The surfacing of the square, while seemingly delicate and aesthetic, provides a solid base for events and activities, which also take place outside museum opening times in the grounds. [mh]

Programme Design of the outdoor spaces of an art museum **Designer** Schønherr A/S **Commissioned by** Herning Center of the Arts Project Foundation **Area** 2.1 ha **Design** 2006–2008 **Implementation** 2008-2009 **Budget** € 430,000 (surrounding landscape)

Paving detail.

Ground plan.

The concrete in the underpass has been clad with corten steel mesh. Photo Jure Erzen

Along the promenade between Ljubljana town hall and the castle in Tivoli Park, the underpass at the level of the Museum of Modern Art is an important connection. At this point the cycle- and foot-path crosses a wide traffic artery consisting of a main road and a railway line. The long underpass was badly neglected for many decades, making a walk between the park and the city centre both unpleasant and unsafe. The paving was broken, railings were loose, the underpass stank of sewage and vandals and graffiti artists had a free rein. Under the renovations the underpass was cleaned up, lighting was installed, the steps and paving were repaired, wooden seating was placed in the recesses and the concrete pillars were clad with 'anti-graffiti' corten steel mesh. The result is an accessible and pleasant urban space – where the raw presence of the heavy and noisy infrastructure is still tangible: the concrete pillars are still visible through the corten steel mesh. That graffiti artists have had to seek refuge elsewhere is regrettable, but this is far outweighed by the improvements to this important pedestrian and cycle connection in the city. [mh]

Programme Renovation of an underpass between city centre and Tivoli Park **Designer** prostoRoz **Commissioned by** Ljubljana Tourist Board **Area** 927 m² **Design** 2009 **Implementation** 2009 **Budget** € 240,000

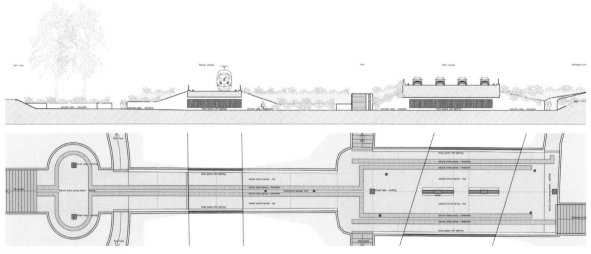

Ground plan and section.

TIVOLI UNDERPASS designed by prostoRoz

KATZENBACH CENTRAL SQUARE

designed by Robin Winogrond Landschaftsarchitekten

Landscape design for the external space in Katzenbach, a new residential estate in Zurich.

At first glance the design of the central square of Katzenbach, a new residential development on the edge of Zurich seems to be purely decorative. The ground surface displays abstract forms, which contrast with the sober and modest architecture of the housing complexes. But behind this apparently random pattern lies an atmospheric design concept into which a dense structure of functions has been subtly integrated. Further enquiry reveals that the gravel and concrete forms on the ground of the plaza are inspired by the shadow pattern that is created when sunlight falls through the trees' leaf cover – as well as the patterns of movement. The morphology of the design is restrained and consists simply of three materials and two colours. The result is a flowing pattern of light concrete paths, areas of gravel and varying shades of greens in a tree palette of robinia, pine and ash. The playful design of the central plaza complements the simple and more severely landscaped courtyards. Thus the plaza really adds to the district and it is an attractive space for residents, playing children and passers-by. [mh]

Programme Design of a square in a new residential estate **Designer** Robin Winogrond Landschaftsarchitekten **In collaboration with** Zita Cotti Architekten (housing, pavilion) **Commissioned by** Housing Cooperative Glattal Zurich **Area** 0.13 ha **Design** 2008–2009 **Implementation** 2010 **Budget** € 255,000

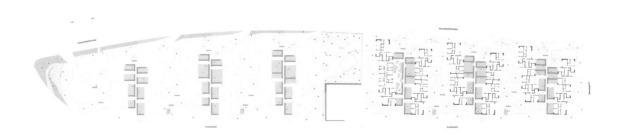

Landscape design for the external space in the new residential estate Katzenbach. The square is in the middle.

BERN

Experiencing nature at your doorstep. All photos Christian Schwager

HARDEGG RESIDENTIAL AREA

designed by Rotzler Krebs Partner

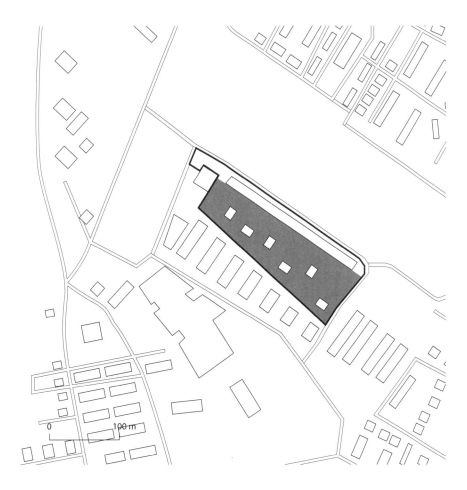

JURY COMMENT Hardegg is an outstanding example of topography and water combined with a highly built-up residential area, of compact urban housing with a loose open landscape. This project is striking for its contrasts, skilfully mastered from the first urban planning concept down to the last construction detail: the dense housing volumes allowing for a vast open space, formally shaped islands scattered into the expanse of an informal meadow, precise functional spaces alternating with multi-use stretches, a strict water system irrigating an evolving creek landscape. This landscape is natural but not a wilderness, rough and yet accessible, and low cost in terms of maintenance.

Ground plan.

Section. The green carpet extends partly onto a car park.

Design allowing for natural processes

Feature by Claudia Moll

Nutrient-poor grassland lies to the front of the long residential building on the Hardegg estate, a housing association development at the southern edge of Bern. The grass also grows all around the six detached multistorey houses on the estate. A narrow meadow stream flows peacefully along its south-eastern boundary. Visitors may wonder whether the grassy field had already developed before the houses were built on the fallow land at the edge of town. Is the stream a relic of bygone days when farms stood here and cattle grazed? Were the buildings planted against this idyllic natural backdrop – or was it the other way around? What is artificial here, and what is natural?

The starting point of the estate, which was inaugurated in 2009, is Rappardplatz. A circular fountain rises out of the asphalt, surrounded by circular spaces in which pines grow, the edges of which form circular benches. The new access road and traffic-calmed street that mark the boundary of the grounds on its north-eastern side can be reached from here. White spots are painted on the tarmac paths leading through the seven-storey block to the detached multistorey houses. The circular shapes recur on the grass in the form of round stepping stones of light coloured concrete and come together to form paths that meander through the open space, leading to large platforms that are also round in shape. Featuring playground equipment and a broad concrete strip, these islands protrude above the grass carpet or sink into it. One is in the bed of the stream; the water flows over another deeper-set concrete ring. The recurrent circles of different sizes already bear witness to the artificiality of the installations, and any remaining doubt in the visitor's mind is removed upon seeing the transverse sides of the long site: the water from the meadow stream emerges into daylight from a precisely moulded concrete structure and disappears at the other end into a similar construction.

Two formerly diametrically opposed camps seem to be reconciled in the Hardegg residential area. Nature versus design was a hot topic on the Swiss landscape architectural scene in the 1980s. Advocates of the natural garden movement called for more nature in the city in response to the rapid changes that followed the construction boom of the time. Opponents criticized the open spaces arising in this manner as being 'pseudonatural' and accused the designers of romantic notions and denial of reality. Their position was that human interventions should be recognisable as such; in the words of the design-based landscape architect Dieter Kienast, the main priority was 'the principle of the readability of the world'. The lake designed by the landscape architect agency Stern und Partner and environmental designer Eduard Neuenschwander for the Grün 80 garden show in Basel Brügglingen came in for heavy criticism. Not only were the foundations of the seemingly idyllic body of water sealed with bitumen, the water had to be – and still has to be – pumped into the basin because of the geology of the area. With its irregular shoreline demarcated by sandstone blocks, the lake looks like the work of a glacier from the last Ice Age, but was in fact put there to replace fields that had been used intensively for agriculture.

The deceptively naturally meandering Hardegg Sulgenbach stream is an artefact too. Like its counterpart in Basel, it is fed from an artificial source. The stream that was piped underground many years ago cannot flow naturally through this area that was formerly used to mine gravel for processing into precast concrete. A pumping system transports the water to the new riverbed. For energy conservation, the valve is shut off at night. The landscape architects in charge of the project, Rotzler Krebs Partner, modelled the gently sloping topography of the exterior space from variously composed gravel substrates, performing part of the work on the roof of the underground car park attached to the estate. However, in contrast to the natural gardens of the 1980s, the architects wanted the design interventions to be recognisable as such. In other words: no sources hidden beneath rocks, but a right-angled concrete structure from which the water mysteriously gushes forth, and a similar construction at the other end where it audibly disappears underground; stepping stones are white concrete, not sandstone; there are no picturesquely strewn glacial boulders from the excavations, but flat platforms and a commitment to the circle as a geometrical form, which recurs throughout the grounds and speaks an unmistakeable design language. However, the choice of plants is in keeping with the location and reminiscent of a natural garden: native meadow flowers and herbs make for a colourfully blooming area of low-maintenance grassland; willows, poplars, sea-buckthorn shrubs and tamarisks have been scattered into the mix to provide shade, and watercress and marsh marigolds grow in the shallow stream. The landscape architects want to encourage coexistence: the stream is both a spawning location for frogs and a bathing spot for children; butterflies flutter over the species-diverse meadow, but footballs can fly and trail bikes cross it too. The area is designed to withstand the heavy-duty exposure typical of an open space in an urban environment. At the same time, it gives city dwellers proximity to nature as it changes with the seasons and abundant wildlife thrives here.

Besides these principles, this design was also chosen with economic factors in mind. Gravel, low cost in itself, was easily and unfussily brought in using large machinery thanks to the amount of space available. Thus, more planning time and more money for installation was available for the round concrete structures cast on site, the prefabricated stepping-stones, and the structures controlling water flow. As a result, at a price of about € 110 per square metre, the project cost much less than other recent residential environment design projects in Switzerland. The meticulously precise design of the 'hard' elements benefits from the expanse and openness of the overall area. The two apparent antitheses come together in an accomplished whole. The qualities of the development are particularly apparent to the visitor when compared with the environment of the adjacent residential estate, likewise built several years ago. On the other side of the stream, the flowery meadow gives way to a low-maintenance but monotonous area of greenery that has no secrets to yield to explorers. The successful Hardegg-project is founded upon a successfully balanced collaboration between architects and landscape architects. While incorporating a large proportion of the housing units into the 200-metre-long block had been stipulated by the building association, it also enabled apartment blocks with a relatively small surface area to be distributed in the freed-up area, and also yielded enough space for a generously designed environment.

Designer Rotzler Krebs Partner (Stefan Rotzler, Matthias Krebs, Jacques Mennel, Markus Crukowicz, Michael Brogle, Christophe Schubert) **In collaboration with** MattiRagazHitz-Architekten (architecture and overall management) **Commissioned by** Baugenossenschaft Brünnen-Eichholz, Bern (housing association) **Area** 1.95 ha **Design** 2004–2007 **Implementation** 2008–2009 **Budget** € 2,136,500

The circle is a main element of design – round stepping stones form paths.

e artificial Sulgenbach stream meanders gently through the outdoor facilities.

e housing development lies at the southern end of Bern. Rappardplatz is the starting point of the estate.

Tarmac paths with painted white circles lead to the apartment blocks.

The circles are angled so that they serve as benches.

contrast to the formal geometry of the circles, Sulgenbach stream develops formally.

The circle segment reveals the artificiality of the water course.

The banks of the stream and concrete elements are popular hangouts for the estate's younger residents.

Essay by Claudia Moll

Swiss landscape architecture has earned a reputation for its outstanding quality, and the projects that have been regularly honoured by the Landscape Architecture Europe Foundation are evidence of this. In all three award presentations, the Swiss entries were outstandingly numerous in relation to the modest size of this country in the heart of Europe. The juries continue to be impressed by the simplicity of the designs and the power that lies in their restraint, and they applaud the way the landscape architects deal with landscape and integrate projects into it. Can this high standard be attributed to the much cited cliché of Swiss precision or is there more behind it? Let us try to seek out the reasons for the Swiss success.

We soon encounter the first difficulty in our attempt. With four parts of the country, just as many official languages, and the concomitant diversity of cultural identities, Switzerland is hard to comprehend as a unified entity. The 26 partly autonomous cantons into which the country is politically subdivided differ, not least in the ways they handle public space. Add to this the effect of the turbulent topography on the value of the open spaces: over 4,000 people are clustered into each square metre in the flat Mittelland, where green spaces are rare, while the density is fewer than 50 per square metre in the Alpine regions. As a result, there can be no one Swiss landscape architecture as such – or is it exactly these different conditions that mean there is one after all?

One look at the history of Swiss garden design teaches us two things.[1] First of all, Switzerland is not a traditional garden country and, secondly, the roots of Swiss garden culture are not Swiss. Agriculture characterized the – for many centuries not very prosperous – country until the middle of the 20th century. In the confederation of states, apart from a few exceptions, there were few patrons present to commission parks and gardens. Not until the 19th century, when the garden arts had already made history in most European countries, did representatives of the rising middle class take on this role. Because the professional category of horticulturalist did not exist in their own country, the Swiss hired designers from nearby foreign countries for their gardens. Developments paralleled – with a slight time lag – those in the neighbouring countries until the mid-20th century. The 'pioneers', Theodor (1810-1993) and Otto Froebel (1844-1906), as well as Evariste Mertens (1846-1907), designed in the style of late neoclassical landscape gardens and, being owners of commercial nurseries, placed a strong emphasis on plants. This characteristic feature continued in the work of Gustav Ammann (1885-1955), the most important exponent of the architectural reform garden and, later, the 'naturalistic' residential garden style (*Wohngartenstil*).[2]

After World War II, the profession was at a turning point. New responsibilities in urban design had to be faced: the population's leisure activities had changed and called for a new way of dealing with nature; modern infrastructure systems such as motorways had to be integrated into the landscape. Planning projects and large-scale designs were therefore among the new areas of responsibility for professionals who, over time, no longer called themselves garden architects but landscape architects.[3] While this re-orientation was accompanied by a sense of insecurity, it also made way for a new generation of designers, for whom a sculptural-abstract formal idiom superseded the all-important use of plants. Ernst Cramer (1898–1980), Willi Neukom (1917–1983) and Fred Eicher (1927–2010) designed in clear lines, a characteristic feature that also informs the work of today's landscape architects. Cramer's 'The Poet's Garden' (*Garten des Poeten*) with its geometrical forms and almost no flowers – red geraniums grew in only one asbestos cement container – stood the common conception of design on its head. Created on the occasion of the first national horticultural exhibition G|59, this theme garden met with strong criticism from the public. It was cleared away immediately after the exhibition ended and did not gain recognition until much later. Only at the end of the 20th century was it 're-discovered' by professional circles. Today it is considered an icon of modern Swiss garden and park design.[4] Willi Neukom's projects are not quite as reduced as Cramer's and may instead be classified as abstract naturalism.[5] Nevertheless, they are also marked by clear lines and the reduction of materials. The experience of landscape plays a major role in his projects. This is the case with Zürich's lakeshore pathway (*Seeuferweg*), likewise planned for the G|59 but only realized in 1963, which opens up towards the Alpine panorama.[6] Finally, clear design lines and the integration of the surrounding natural landscape are also the main characteristics of work by Fred Eicher, whose Eichbühl Cemetery, built five years later in Zürich Altstetten, seems to grow in understated shapes out of the base of the Uetliberg.

The economic boom that started in the 1960s radically and fundamentally changed the Swiss landscape. The orchard meadows covering the flat Mittelland gave way to large-scale developments, motorways and industrial zones; small intact villages became the suburban communities of urban sprawl, and agriculture that was oriented toward greater yields eliminated the variously structured landscape spaces. Rapid and inexora-

See Annemarie Bucher, n Landschaftsgarten zur Gartandschaft – Schweizerische tengestaltung auf dem Weg ie Gegenwart', in: Archiv für weizer Gartenarchitektur und dschaftsplanung (ed.), Vom dschaftsgarten zur Gartenlschaf: Gartenkunst zwischen '0 und 1980 im Archiv für weizer Gartenarchitektur und dschaftsplanung, 1996, pp. 36.

For the work of Gustav nan, see Johannes Stoffler, tav Ammann: Landschaften Moderne in der Schweiz,)8.

See Peter Wullschleger, 'Was ge währt ist aller Anfang, 75 re BSLA', anthos 39, 2000, 4, pp. 62–65.

See Architekturforum ch (ed.), Garten des Poeten)/2009, 2009, a textbook ompanying the exhibition the same title, 30 April June 2009. For the work rnst Cramer, see Udo lacher, Visionäre Gärten: Die dernen Landschaften von st Cramer, 2001.

See Brigitt Sigel and Erik le Jong, Der Seeuferweg in 'ch: Eine Spazierlandschaft Moderne von 1963, 2010.

Ibid. The G|59 extended all und the bay in Zürich. Willi ikom, in collaboration with st Baumann, was responsifor the design of the exhibi-areas on the right bank.

See Claudia Moll, turgarten – "Lebensraum Biotop"', in Claudia Moll l Axel Simon, Eduard ıenschwander: Architekt und weltgestalter. 2009, pp. 5-187.

Both protagonists lished their opinions in ıks; see Louis Le Roy, uur uitschakelen, Natuur chakelen, 1973; Urs Schwarz, ' Naturgarten: Mehr Platz für heimische Pflanzen and Tiere, 30.

See Anette Freytag, Natur werfen: Zum Werk des weizer Landschafts-hitekten Dieter Kienast 45–1998), Diss. Zürich 11. This dissertation will be ued in revised and expanded n as a book published by gta cooperation with Architectura latura (2013).

ble changes paired with fear for the planet's future led to the birth of environmental movements all over the world, which spread the message that the planet's resources are finite. In the history of gardens and parks this development found expression in the natural garden movement (Naturgartenbewegung), which had strong repercussions not only in the Netherlands and Germany but also in Switzerland.

The Dutch Louis Le Roy and the Swiss Urs Schwarz are considered the fathers of the natural garden movement.[7] While the former stood primarily for the approach that was critical of civilization and propagated the people's participation in the design of their environment, Schwarz, the biologist, argued from an ecological and biological point of view. Neither of them made any statements about design and formal idiom.[8] This was done in Switzerland by another representative of the movement, Eduard Neuenschwander (born in 1924), who studied architecture at Zurich's Polytechnikum and acquired his first professional experience in Alvar Aalto's practice. He was impressed not only by the architecture of the Nordic master – whose influences are clearly visible in his own architectural oeuvre – but also by the broad Finnish landscape with its forests, amorphously shaped lakes and gently contoured topography. Starting in the mid-1970s, Neuenschwander turned away from architecture and from then on devoted his attention to the environmental design of outdoor spaces. His parks and gardens in the urban domain were intended to create refuges – both for plants and animals and for people. Resulting from his holistic world picture and the impact of Finland, his outdoor spaces at first glance had little to do with the clear design of Modernism. In a large number of private gardens and in Irchelpark (in collaboration with Stern and Partner, inaugurated in 1986) gently meandering meadow-covered embankments replaced the accurate geometrical forms. Sandstone blocks terraced the grounds, a multitude of mostly native plants enclosed the individual park spaces, and frogs lived in the natural ponds where human users swam at the same time.

The artificially created idyll pleased the garden owners, not least because they could thus actively contribute to improving the living environment. In specialized professional circles, however, this kind of design met with criticism; here it was considered pseudo-nature and window dressing. One of its most vehement opponents was Dieter Kienast (1945–1998), still young at the time. After his apprenticeship as a gardener in Zürich, Kienast studied landscape and open space planning at the Gesamthochschule Kassel and subsequently, during his first years of work as a landscape architect, he completed his doctorate in the specialized field of plant sociology.[9] Kienast sharply criticized what he saw as pseudo-scientific theories of

ART OR NATURE - A SWISS DEBATE

The Poet's Garden, 1959. Photo Schweizerische Stiftung für Landschaftsarchitektur SLA, Rapperswil

Zurich's lakeshore pathway, 1963. Photo Schweizerische Stiftung für Landschaftsarchitektur SLA, Rapperswil

Eichbühl Cemetery, 1968. Photo André Melchior

Irchelpark, 1986. Photo Archiv Hochbauamt des Kantons Zürich

Brühlwiese, 1984. Photo Anette Freytag, 2011

| See Dieter Kienast, 'Vom
urnahen Garten oder von der
zbarkeit der Vegetation', *Der
tenbau* 100, 1979, no. 25,
117-122.

| See 'Form als Antithese
x Naturgarten: Der Stadt-
k Brühlwiese in Wettingen
79–1983)', in Freytag (as in
e 9), pp. 193-223.

| See footnote 10.

| See Hans-Ulrich Weber, 'Die
eilung Grünplanung, Land-
afts- und Gartenarchitektur
Interkantonalen Technikum
perswil', *anthos*, 1980, no.
p. 12-15. So far, the study
andscape architecture is
v possible in Rapperswil
chschule Rapperswil HSR)
Geneva (Haute École
genieurs du paysage HEPIA)
he Fachhochschule level
llege of Applied Sciences);
e is no university-level study
gramme.

the advocates of the natural garden movement and he encouraged his profession to think about what they were doing. Even though he too denounced the constant environmental deterioration and the monotony of the open spaces created at the time, he rejected the exclusive line of argument and the 'pastoral tone' of the supporters of the natural garden movement.[10]

The study of spontaneous vegetation led Kienast to new aesthetics for the design of nature in the city. Unlike that of the natural garden movement's advocates, it was not to copy images of nature but to be an element in its own right. The manifesto of this approach is considered to be Brühlwiese, a city park planned by Kienast for the municipality of Wettingen from 1979 and inaugurated in 1984.[11] By citing elements from different garden design eras in a postmodern manner and combining them into a whole with axes and avenues as in a Baroque garden, he re-established the work of landscape architects in a cultural context. 'The Poet's Garden' too was revived here. Instead of flower borders, the park's entrance area featured slim, scaffold-like steel structures overgrown with climbing plants, and the hills for sledding that the client had requested became accurately shaped pyramids of earth – but, unlike Cramer's geometrically formed hills, these were covered with flowery calcareous grassland.

The conflict between two different camps promoting more or less naturalness in garden and park design is nothing new in the history of gardens – the last version of this debate had taken place towards the end of the 19th century. The one that ignited in Switzerland at the end of the 1970s, however, should be rated as an important milestone for the profession in that country. When Kienast called for approaching the necessary 'renewal of the culture of gardens [...] not [as] a formal problem but [as] one of content',[12] he asked his professional colleagues to recall their roots and become completely clear about their work. The debate about naturalness versus artificiality also influenced the landscape architects trained in this period and was reflected in their work. As professors, exponents of both camps left their mark on the course of study in landscape architecture at the Interkantonal Technikum in Rapperswil, which had been founded a little earlier in 1972. This is a rather technically oriented, very circumscribed educational institution where as late as 1980 only 35 students were enrolled in the whole programme.[13] The two professors of garden and landscape design facing each other in Rapperswil were Dieter Kienast and Christian Stern, whose practice Stern and Partner pursued a fairly ecological direction. Many of their students later became colleagues and principals of Swiss firms that are renowned today. The engagement with the tension between the poles of art, nature and the temporal dimension is visible in their work – at first in a very severe and almost overdone form, now in a self-confident idiom in which the former antitheses have become reconciled. The work of Rotzler Krebs Partner, whose landscaping of the *Hardegg residential area* and *Brühlgutpark* are featured in this book, are one example of this new self-assurance. An interest in the history of place without losing sight of today's users is just as present in their work as a treatment that attributes equal value to design and ecological concerns.

As in most European countries, in Switzerland too today's generation of landscape architects faces a new challenge in the increasing amalgamation of city and countryside. From now on, teamwork with planners in various disciplines and the ability to handle large-scale dimensions are what is required. To enable landscape architects to put forward their concerns and requests as partners with equal rights, educational opportunities need to be broadened. A Master's program is still lacking in Switzerland. Only with postgraduate education can the new responsibilities be tackled with the same seriousness in future and the high standards of Swiss landscape architecture maintained.

Claudia Moll, joint editor of this edition of Landscape Architecture Europe, is a landscape architect and writes about landscape architecture.

ARTIFICIAL NATURE

REYKJAVIK

TULLAMORE

AMSTERDAM
ESSEN

LAUSANNE

BILBAO **CADAQUÉS**

BEGUR
BARCELONA

Highlighting the basement rock.

CAP DE CREUS

designed by Estudi Martí Franch and Ardevols Associats

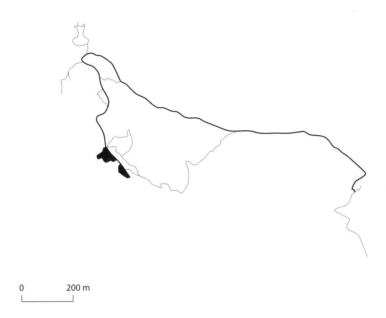

0   200 m

JURY COMMENT The originality of this project relies on the courageous attitude of the public client to remove an acclaimed architectural complex of holiday homes from the coast it exploited for tourism - and therefore also maintained in economic terms. In giving priority to nature over human settlement, the Catalan administration has introduced a new understanding of the leisure landscape of Cap de Creus, inviting a more transient human presence. What could have become a banal nature restoration project has evolved into an extraordinary landscape project through the attitude of the designers, who skilfully construe and orchestrate the de-construction as a combination of de-struction and con-struction. Their way of dismantling the buildings and reusing the debris, as well as their site-affective composition of a framework of access roads, paths and observation platforms is as accommodating of natural processes as it is of human practices.

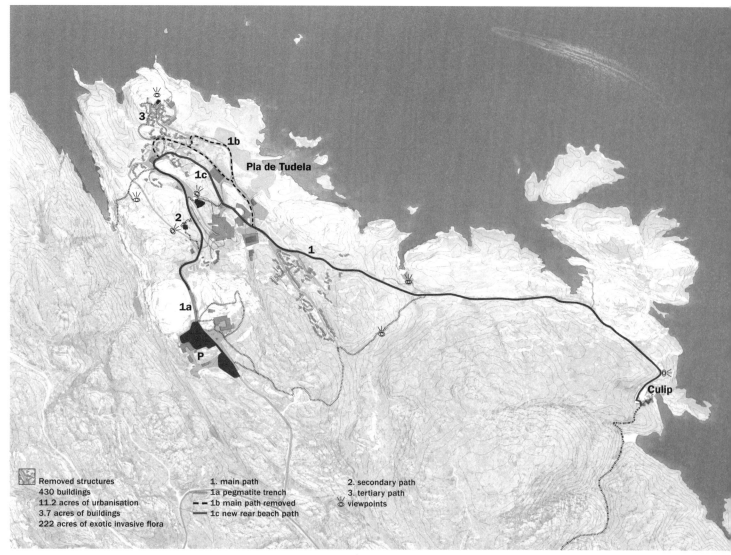

Map showing the design interventions.

Removed structures
430 buildings
11.2 acres of urbanisation
3.7 acres of buildings
222 acres of exotic invasive flora

1. main path
1a pegmatite trench
1b main path removed
1c new rear beach path

2. secondary path
3. tertiary path
viewpoints

Final situation.

Conceiving the conditions for nature at work

Feature by Thierry Kandjee

Situated between the Vermilion Coast and the Bay of Rosas to the east of the Albera mountain range, Cap de Creus is an area renowned for its unique geological and botanical heritage. Its rocky coast, regularly punctuated by tiny inlets, is the result of thousands of years of incessant wave action, mainly due to the northerly/north-westerly Tramontane wind and winds from the east. Remarkable geological outcrops are one of the most distinctive features of this natural space. The forms and patterns of the geological landscape have excited the imagination of visitors and residents for centuries, among them Salvador Dali. The exceptional nature of the site prompted the construction in 1961 of Club Med Tudela, an innovative tourist complex designed by the architects Pelayo Martínez and Jean Weiler. This project was recognized as being one of the most remarkable developments on the Spanish coast in its reconciliation of landscape with modern architecture. Classification of the Cap de Creus site as a natural park in 1998 heralded the end of the holiday village's operations. It was closed down in 2003 and its planned demolition marked the start of the restoration project conceived of by Estudi Martí Franch (EMF) and the office of Ardevols Associats (AA).

The project presented here is about the transformation of this human settlement into a protected space of great value for tourism. Far from being a simple bid to restore the site's ecological dynamics, the project contributes towards an exploration of new ways of managing a coastal environment that has all too often been abandoned to the forces of property markets. To French tourists, the Tudela holiday village offered the prospect of a way of life integrated with nature, typical of its time. Today, Cap de Creus Natural Park has become a popular location for scuba diving and hiking on a national scale, representing the largest exploited segment of the Mediterranean coast in Catalonia. This project, the framework conditions of which are exceptional in the Spanish context in particular, is rooted in a two-fold political move: the classification of a very large coastal area of prime real estate as a protected area, and the

demolition of a complex of building settlements acclaimed for their architectural significance.

The challenge in restoring the site resides in three issues that have been skilfully addressed by EMF&AA. The landscape architects decided early on to combine demolition of the existing buildings with conservation of the site. They calculated that demolition of the holiday complex would in addition generate a quantity of debris that could be used as material for the project. Another major concern for EMF&AA, in their bid to encourage biodiversity, was to eradicate the invasive Crassulaceae species, mostly Hottentot Fig (Carpobrotus edulis) planted by the Club Med developers but now identified as an invasive species in specialized coastal habitats. Last but not least, the landscape architects sought a means to absorb the growing pressure of tourism on the site, which attracts a quarter of a million visitors a year.

By establishing a specific means of intervention for each building typology, the response developed by EMF&AA aimed to reduce the road infrastructure to the elements necessary for use of the site to its best advantage, to restore the ecological, hydrographic and orographic dynamics, and to direct movement between locations. The designers' main action was to devise a system to organize and manage visitor flows on the site while identifying the site's capacity to receive the public in view of the quality of experience on offer. Three route typologies were therefore proposed, starting from the parking space at the entrance, which has been redesigned on the basis of the existing lot. The elimination of incoming motorized traffic is part of the principal site conservation strategy. First, the main asphalt roads to be used by the Natural Park's staff extend for 2 km and reuse the existing roads while downsizing their width. Second, the secondary network of concrete paths leads to dedicated belvederes. Third, minimal interventions, such as 'landmarks', invite visitors to engage with the landscape beyond roads and paths. As for the belvederes, the landscape architects have created two types of observation platforms designed specifically to experience this landscape. The first enable viewers to observe the maritime environment and re-use existing building foundations, and the second encourage appreciation of the site's geological features. In that sense, EMF's approach is based on the narratives and other interpretations that artists, fishermen and children have made of the landscape.

One of the special features of this project is the didactic approach developed by EMF&AA. What started out as a demolition order, a strictly technical brief, evolved into a creative landscape project. The methodology adopted by EMF&AA constitutes a conduit, an open process based on precise cartography of the materials of the site undergoing demolition. The project in its entirety benefited from the expertise of over 50 disciplines specialized in the restoration of natural, geological and marine environments and dynamics. In this process, the landscape architects played the role of knowledge coordinators and synthesizers throughout the conceptualization process. The essential genius of the project rests in recognizing the site's capacity to recolonize the land after deconstruction. The next thrust of the landscape architects' approach was to structure the access routes. The approach is one of facilitation: helping the site to recover its orographic system and enabling the various disciplines to work in concert. In a way, the attitude of the designers was just as important as their aesthetic choices.

This project is directly related to an important aspect of what landscape architecture is about, namely identifying and fitting in with what is already there. According to Martí Franch, EMF director, the project does not set out to build landscape but to conceive the conditions for experiencing landscape. To do so, the most interesting development stage in the project involved in-depth site reconnaissance activity. During the 14 months of construction, the EMF&AA team walked more than 200km within the site in search of ways to choreograph on-site visitors. This phase allowed those involved to draw inspiration on site. As an example, the reconstruction of the pegmatite route opened up ways to interact with the in-situ basement rock. Franch's original idea was to uncover the whole path and expose the basement rock by stripping the existing paved route. The discovery during the construction process that the rock was too fragile prompted the landscape professional to think up an alternative approach. He unveiled the specific stratigraphy of the rocks which he chose to highlight and reinforce by using 'in situ' formulated concrete flooring, thus enabling a play on contrasts in texture and revealing the rock.

Beyond mere restoration to a former natural state that would be impossible to achieve, EMF's approach aimed for skilful de-construction of the existing buildings. The EMF project construes nature as the creation of interactions between natural phenomena and site practices. This approach embraces all the ambiguity of landscape architecture as a process of design and artifice. The Tudela project is an innovative response to a remarkable commission that gives priority to nature over this privileged space. It demonstrates mastery in the field of restoration and revitalizes the recognized expertise of the Catalonian landscape architects.

Programme Landscape restoration **Designer** Estudi Martí Franch and Ardevols Associats **Commissioned by** Spanish Ministry of the Environment, Rural and Marine Affairs Catalan Department of Environment Gestora de Runes de la Construcció SL **Area** 200 ha **Design** 2005–2009 **Implementation** 2009–2010 **Budget** €7,000,000

The tourist complex of Club Med before the intervention.

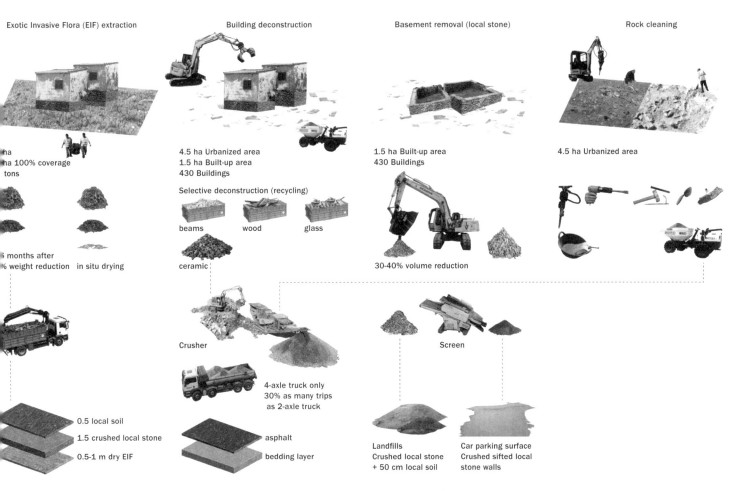

Exotic Invasive Flora (EIF) extraction

ha
ha 100% coverage
tons

months after
% weight reduction   in situ drying

0.5 local soil
1.5 crushed local stone
0.5-1 m dry EIF

Building deconstruction

4.5 ha Urbanized area
1.5 ha Built-up area
430 Buildings

Selective deconstruction (recycling)

beams   wood   glass

ceramic

Crusher

4-axle truck only
30% as many trips
as 2-axle truck

asphalt
bedding layer

Basement removal (local stone)

1.5 ha Built-up area
430 Buildings

30-40% volume reduction

Screen

Landfills
Crushed local stone
+ 50 cm local soil

Car parking surface
Crushed sifted local
stone walls

Rock cleaning

4.5 ha Urbanized area

...ocess of the demolition of the holiday village and the reconstruction of the natural coastline.

...moving Club Med and restoring the coastline.

Asphalt road to cope with the flow of visitors.

Observation platforms.

Concrete path encouraging exploration of the site.

htweight construction for safety and marking.

Existing buildings are reused as observation platforms.

Essay by Maria Hellström

PERFORM WITH NATURE

What is 'the place of nature in the city of man'? Contemporary landscape architecture proposes several answers. One, of which the *Vondelpark Canopy Walk* in Amsterdam is an example, is delivered in the form of an urban woodland, enacted through multisensory walking. Another, the *Sculpture Park Boora Bog* in Tullamore, Ireland, is presented as an excavated yet abandoned peat marshland, now re-activated through differentiated maintenance. A third, here exemplified by Anouk Vogel's temporary installations *A Chaque Château son Jardin (Garden on castle square)* and *Cacticity Urban garden*, is offered in the form of a challenging of representative urbanity through excessive cultivation. And finally a fourth, the *Mechtenberg fields* with the pertinent title *Utilitas et venustas*, 'useful and delightful', emerges as the re-programming of an agro-industrial field, re-enchanted through colourful cyclic growth. Nature is being recognized it seems, as an immanent field of forces, a mesh of transformative energies, an influential matter of fact, which, at least in theory, should be acknowledged as something more than a green rim on the horizon.

Although frequently addressed, the question, which was originally posed by the renowned landscape architect and environmentalist Ian McHarg half a decade ago, still demands attention. What is the current place of nature in an increasingly urbanized world? Conventionally, the place of man in relation to nature has been a given. The progressive position has been 'on top' or 'ahead' of nature that has been degraded to a repository for sewage, a locus for expressways or a site for asphalted playgrounds. McHarg obviously wanted to challenge this assumption. Is there room for nature in the civil structures that humans have created for themselves? Or have we reached a point where it is necessary to explicitly justify nature's presence in order for it to remain?

There are very few notions that are so central, yet so evasive, as nature. Nature is a concept connoting essential qualities and innate dispositions; the cosmological course of things, of life and death. Etymologically, 'nature' has to do with the Latin *nasci*, to be born, a phenomenon as shared as anything can ever be, yet as incomprehensible. While nature seems to constitute the fundament of our being, it also refers to groundbreaking impulses or creative powers; forces that are not only basic but eruptive and unpredictable, and as such, preconditions for differentiation and change.

The initial question of McHarg, raised in an article in 1964 and further developed in the influential inquiry *Design With Nature* of 1969, not only actualized the existential relationship between man and the environment. It also brought to our attention the means we develop in order to handle, reflect upon and develop this relationship in more or less meaningful ways. As a rhetorical figure, the question also made us aware of the concepts, languages and signifying practices we set up in order to approach the topic – in short the design actions that constitute the complex interface between our surroundings and ourselves. McHarg was very aware of this, and therefore deliberately gave his question a rhetorical twist. At the same time, he was careful to underline that his pretentious inquiry was meant to be "neither ironic nor facetious but of the utmost urgency and seriousness".[1]

A re-reading of McHarg today is as fascinating as it is necessary. In many ways, McHarg was ahead of his time. Well aware of the importance of an expanded discourse, he was early in developing interdisciplinary landscape courses, and in 1960 he even hosted his own TV show, *The House We Live In*; a deliberate attempt to introduce ecological thinking to a broader audience.[2] The shaping of our common *oikos*, our shared home or habitat, argued McHarg, should depend on more than just rational functionality. A highway is not simply a structural element linking two points in a grid, but also an explicit landscape gesture actively interfering with the manifold system of processes in which it is uttered. It is a transformative and significant act with far-reaching, social and cultural effects, all of which should be carefully explored, mapped out and superimposed, the one onto the other. A complex and dynamic environment requires an equally multifaceted and flexible working method in order to make sense.

McHarg's inquiry placed a new emphasis on the inescapable complexity of human-environmental interaction, but also, and perhaps more importantly, highlighted the means and measures that we develop in order to handle it. To design with nature, for McHarg, meant acting both beyond instrumental problem-solving and 'bleeding-heartism',[3] in close response to the cyclic workings of hydrosphere, atmosphere and lithosphere. Although McHarg's bio-centric approach in this sense reflected a scientific mind-set, he still chose to define his empirical and adaptive method as 'design'. We may ask why. Is not design an utterly anthropocentric and, from nature's perspective, inevitably detrimental activity? While the immediate answer would be affirmative, it is, however, not a given. Although an ordering activity, design is always situated and context dependent. If we re-evaluate nature, we evidently need to reconsider also our re-ordering of it. A new ontology, or a new understanding of the

J.L. Austin, *How to Do Things with Words*, 1962.

H. Bergson, *Creative Evolution*, 1911/2001.

J. Butler, *Excitable Speech: Politics of the Performative*, 1997.

Felix Guattari, *Three Ecologies*, 2000.

Ian McHarg, 'The place of nature in the City of Man' in *Annals of the American Academy of Political and Social Science*, Vol. 2, March 1964, pp 1-12.

Ian McHarg, *Design with Nature*, 1969/1992.

Jacques Rancière, *The Politics of Aesthetics*, 2004.

world, requires a new aesthetics, a new framework for qualitatively assessing the same.

McHarg's ecological turn has been extremely influential and continues to be so. But what are the aesthetic implications? To a certain extent, McHarg avoids the question of aesthetics by bending it towards ethics; a twist that also motivates the more scientific approach. It also entails the translation of aesthetic beauty into 'fitness'. Just as evolution, design is a matter of creating fitness. Ecologically speaking, 'fit' involves "the assumption of the environment's provisions of opportunity for the organisms."[4] As such, nature's striving for fitness is not always competitive, favouring the strongest, but as much a matter of enabling interdependence and energy exchange. Referring to environmentalist Aldo Leopold, McHarg articulates his ethical credo: ecologically as well as philosophically, ethics originates in "the tendency of interdependent individuals and groups to evolve modes of cooperation"[5] – processes that in ecology are referred to in terms of *symbioses*.

Ascribing to nature an ethics or a higher purpose, which simply remains to be translated into an appropriate symbolic form, is problematic, suggesting as it does that there is a natural or given solution to the problem of conviviality or systemic complexity. Yet, it is possible to interpret McHarg's ecologically informed design approach in less idealizing and more agency-oriented terms. While attempting to justify design in terms of an 'intercellular altruism',[6] McHarg also draws on more radical versions of ecology, where living matter is seen as fundamentally transitory, already irritable and contractile, continuously open to the influence of external stimulation, and sensitive to mechanical, physical and chemical reactions.[7] What is important is not certain privileged forms and identities, but the very conditions for transformation and differentiation; not the meanings of certain constellations, but the very emergence, exchange and circulation of that which potentially makes sense.

A focus on ecological performance as a complex, materialized distribution and exchange of energy could potentially shed light also on the complexity of human sense-making or aesthetic performance. From an ecological point of view, ordinary linguistic action unfolds as a complex system of speech acts. Simple utterances are not always representative or 'constative',[8] but very often affective or energetic, bodily materialized, guttural sounds, potentially injurious, irritating, imperative or questioning; sayings that cannot be understood outside of the specific speech situation. Other human forms of expression materialize in similar context-dependent ways, always reconfiguring the environment in which they appear.

Rather than twisting the performance of nature towards ethics, we should perhaps acknowledge its close affinity with the field of aesthetics, with the distribution and exchange of the experiential, the affective or the sensible. Nature appears to be the intermediary, where meanings may be renegotiated and spatial relationships reconfigured. As such, the way we understand nature also has consequences for the way we develop our social systems, our urban agglomerations, or our cities. It reminds us of the fact that, as the site of distribution of resources and exchange of energies, nature is also a principal site of political struggle, or of struggle for recognition; a site where fitness, as far as it is at all appropriate, should be used as a means to acknowledge also that which is not fit.

While it is more important than ever to recognize McHarg's imperative to design with nature, to engage in environmentally concerned sense-making, it is also vital to *perform with nature*, to consider the affective role of nature's performances, in aesthetic as well as political terms. As our understanding of ecological performance has increased, it has also become increasingly clear that it unsettles our taken-for-granted ideas of cooperation, interdependence and development. Many landscape projects today clearly address this provocative complexity of the human-nature relationship, materializing bonds and affiliations that would otherwise remain imperceptible. Yet, while some designs settle for the representation of the relatively stable or symbiotic, others take on the challenge of addressing also the disturbing, the parasitic, and the mutational, including the very questionable role of human interference, such as the *Museum courtyard installation*, Martha Schwartz' extremist trickery in Reykjavik. While some projects confine themselves to affirming nature's otherness with established means, others, like Martí Franch's *Cap de Creus* at Cadaqués, Spain, seek to engage in or practise 'the wild'; trying out a position for man as 'the enzyme'[9] of the material world.

Maria Hellström Reimer is professor of design in theory and practice at Malmö University, She is also the director of studies at the Swedish Faculty for Design Research at the

VONDELPARK CANOPY WALK

designed by Carve

The playground engages the park's existing capital, namely the old trees.

The need for an exciting play area in the nineteenth-century Vondelpark would not have been met by installing predictable climbing frames and other play equipment. Instead, a wooden walkway has been created among the treetops, high above the park's paths. On the ground, enough space remains for the many visitors who use this Amsterdam park for many different purposes. The playground fascinates because it engages the park's existing capital, namely the old trees, while very modestly disappearing in them, and therefore delivering a play adventure of a kind that no newly added play equipment would ever be able to provide. The adventurous canopy walk leads children – or anyone who dares – over a series of tower-like platforms and 'swinging' rope bridges. Especially in the summer, when the walkway is overgrown with leaves, the canopy walk feels like a journey through the world of nature. Hidden between branches and leaves, the route passes through a series of secret hideaways and, for a few moments, children escape from the bustle of the city park below. [mh]

Programme Canopy walk in an existing park **Designer** Carve (Elger Blitz, Mark van der Eng, Jasper van der Schaaf, Lucas Beukers) **In collaboration with** Quirijn Verhoog, Arno Heemskerk **Commissioned by** City of Amsterdam **Area** 0.1 ha **Design** 2009–2010 **Implementation** 2010 **Budget** € 180,000

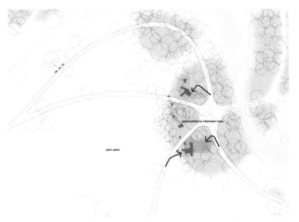

Plan.

In summer the canopy walk feels like a journey through the world of nature.

Cacticity: an open interpretation of the garden-urban dialectic. Photo Jeroen Musch

More than a thousand cacti ranging in height from ten centimetres to one metre were used to compose an incongruous section of landscape in the square adjoining the Bilbao Museum of Fine Arts. Established as part of the Bilbao urban garden festival, this enigmatic place was not designed to be walked upon; rather, it compels recognition as a tactile space to be explored visually. With her play on mineral-plant contrasts, textures, contours, and levels, Anouk Vogel presents us with an open interpretation of the garden-urban dialectic by appropriating the classical language of the garden in a fresh new way. In this 'Cacticity' the landscape architect demonstrates her inventive and playful use of plants as a medium. [tk]

Programme Temporary installation on an urban square **Designer** Anouk Vogel **Commissioned by** Fundación Bilbao 700 - III Millenium Fundazioa **Area** 80m² **Design** 2008 **Implementation** 2009 **Budget** € 6,000

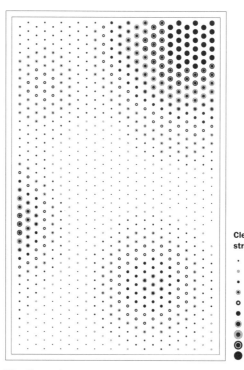

Cleistocactus straussi:

- · 10 cm
- ∘ 20 cm
- • 30 cm
- ⦿ 40 cm
- ○ 50 cm
- ● 60 cm
- ◉ 70 cm
- ◎ 80 cm
- ◉ 90 cm
- ● 100 cm

Planting scheme.

M CHTENBERG FIELDS

designed by Studio Bürgi

Strips of cornflowers and chamomile create a visual spectacle.

Since the creation of the IBA Emscher Park in the industrial landscape of the Ruhr area, some of the agricultural land on the slopes of the Mechtenberg has been protected by turning it into a 'landscape' park. Several seasonal interventions were developed over a period of two years, where specially composed mixtures of flowers were sown in the cornfields, following the agricultural calendar of sowing, growing and harvesting. Flowers such as the common corncockle, marigold, chamomile and cornflower start by forming fine colourful lines, which turn into multi-coloured strips in combination with the grain in nuanced oat fields, and finally into chequered patterns. The selection committee described the project 'Utilitas and Venustas' by studio Bürgi as an original and powerful intervention, made to emphasize the relationship between productive agricultural land and urban surroundings that has almost disappeared. Even though urban dwellers stand at a distance – the visual spectacle is only visible from roads and paths along the edges – the agricultural lands regain meaning by combining agricultural patterns and processes (utilitas) and experimental composition and experiences (venustas), rather than being transformed into a conventional park. According to the jury the project shows the value of fields – precisely by not selling out to urban developers. [mh]

Visualization of the colour patterns.

Programme Temporary planting scheme for Landschaftspark Mechtenberg **Designer** Paolo L. Bürgi, Studio Bürgi (Chiara Pradel, Florentine Schmidt) **Commissioned by** Regionalverband Rhein-Ruhr and Udo Weilacher (curator) **Area** 45 ha **Design** 2008-2010 **Implementation** 2008-2010 (temporary interventions) **Budget** € 80,000

The floral motif transforms the castle square into a poetic and ephemeral public space. Photos Jeroen Musch

designed by Anouk Vogel

GARDEN ON CASTLE SQUARE

Created for the Lausanne garden festival, Anouk Vogel's intervention transforms the existing car park on the castle square into a poetic and ephemeral public space, thereby re-qualifying its context. Inspired by a medieval floral motif, the landscape architect created a clever subversion of the codes and traditions of parterre work and exhibited it in a public space. The space created by this minimal intervention, with its astutely designed polyethylene borders, presents a floral choreography that invites locals and tourists to take a stroll. The castle staircase in that way becomes both a viewing point and a waiting point from which the square reveals itself. The change of use and experience was designed for the duration of the festival and was a response to a matter of local contention: by temporarily removing the car park from the square, the design proved that this did not result in the loss of clients that the shop keepers had feared, while it did create a successful new public space. [tk]

A playful space to walk through.

Programme Temporary installation on a car park **Designer** Anouk Vogel **Commissioned by** Association Jardin Urbain **Area** 0.207 ha **Design** 2008 **Implementation** 2009 **Budget** € 30,000

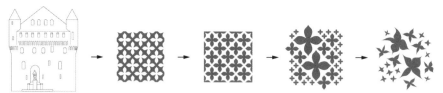

Principle of the project: deconstruction of a medieval ornament. The motif is based on the original stone carvings that adorn the interior walls of the castle.

MUSEUM COURTYARD INSTALLATION
designed by Martha Schwartz

The reflective aluminium surface examines our limited use of natural resources.

The installation in the courtyard of the Museum of Modern Art in Reykjavik represents an invitation to a visual exploration of a large space of unfiltered interception of the natural light that is so distinctive in this part of the world. A closer look reveals that the reflective aluminium surface examines another limit: that of our use of natural resources. Martha Schwartz's intervention 'I hate nature' acts as a provocation developed on the basis of the terms nature/culture/resources. On the boundary between landscape and art, she also questions the limits of landscape architectural intervention – which led to a discussion of the following question among the jury: which oeuvres qualify as landscape architecture? This project points in innovative directions towards an unexplored space that receives little attention in current landscape architectural practice. [tk]

Programme Temporary Installation in the courtyard of an art museum **Designer** Martha Schwartz **Commissioned by** Reykjavik Art Museum **Area** 196m² **Design** 2008 **Implementation** 2008 **Budget** € 105,000

The temporary installation in the courtyard of the Reykjavik Museum of Modern Art.

A space of unfiltered interception of the distinctive natural light.

The artwork 'Raised Circle', by Maurice McDonagh, installed on the flat peat bog. Photo Kevin O'Dwyer

The same artwork five years later in a landscape transformed by succession.

The Boora Bog Complex is an extensive peat bog area in the Irish county of Offaly where the commercial harvesting of peat has ended. Water was previously extracted through drainage and this brought about a flat landscape with a characteristic grid structure. Nowadays, other agents shape the former industrial land, namely forestry, agriculture, tourism, transport, new industrial activities and art. The organization Sculpture in the Parklands, in need of a spatial concept for its grounds that host various outdoor sculptures and art events, commissioned Dermot Foley Landscape Architects to implement a convincingly straightforward landscape strategy based on the management of succession: depending on the type of former peat extraction, some zones have been completely cleared of vegetation to reveal the black peaty substrate, others have remained untouched, thereby allowing for spontaneous vegetation. The jury appreciated how industrial heritage and natural processes are negotiated here in order to create changing spatial situations for existing and future art works. [Id]

Programme Landscape strategy for a sculpture park
Designer Dermot Foley Landscape Architects (Dermot Foley, Bernie Kinsella) **Commissioned by** Sculpture in the Parklands and Offaly County Council **Area** 40 ha
Design 2008 **Implementation** 2010, continuing in phases depending on budget **Budget** 1 €/m²

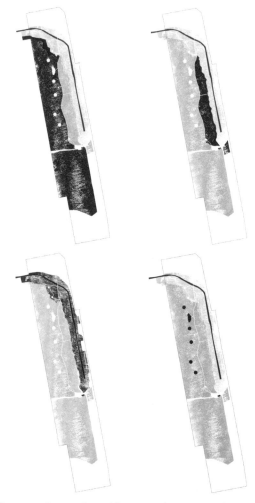

The grounds are shaped by managing succession. From top left to bottom right: non-intervention areas, areas with annual selective tree removal, area where all trees are removed biennially, areas maintained free of vegetation.

A CONCEPTUAL EXPANSION OF PUBLIC SPACE

Essay by Maria Goula

Landscape is probably one of the most popular contemporary cultural paradigms that have had a profound influence on disciplines related to the study and design of the environment during the last decades. Its holistic approach and hybrid nature has encouraged the progressive integration of a new vocabulary related to ecology and sustainability in the language of design. In the Mediterranean, a territory whose narratives are always related to climate and geography but with no tradition in landscape architecture, landscape is the design paradigm *par excellence* that has revolutionized academic curricula, specific literature and practice.

In Catalonia landscape emerged strongly at the beginning of the 1990s. Just after the Olympics, and basking in its worldwide recognition as an urban design laboratory, the city of Barcelona started to be 'viewed' in its metropolitan dimensions as one part of a geographical context: of rivers and streams, mountains, hills and rural remains. Since then Barcelona has rapidly become the capital of a wider landscape movement, a kind of landscape architecture centre in the south of Europe. However, when was this movement born? What are its characteristics? Who were the pioneer figures engaged with landscape as a specific discipline and a challenging profession? And in which context did they operate?

In order to understand Catalan architects' engagement with landscape, one has to look back to the 1980s. The specific know-how on urban design produced during that period represents a sophisticated synergy between strong political will, young and enthusiastic public servants in local administration and, probably most importantly, is a result of the way of teaching that arose in the 1970s at the School of Architecture. In particular, professors like Elias Torres (who was regarded as a kind of spiritual leader by many young designers involved in the design of public space in Barcelona), together with his partner J.A. Martínez-Lapeña, understood the structural role of vegetation in the configuration of the syntax of open space. His notorious article 'Y el resto…. Verde' (And the rest …green)[1] influenced a wide range of architects who were working at that time on the reconstruction of Barcelona and are considered representatives of the landscape collective in Barcelona. It is important to note that landscape architecture as a discipline achieved recognition in the public domain mainly due to a group of designers related to the School of Architecture, who regarded landscape as a fertile terrain for reflective theoretical and research oriented thinking: a natural conceptual expansion of public space.

A CONCEPTUAL EXPANSION OF PUBLIC SPACE

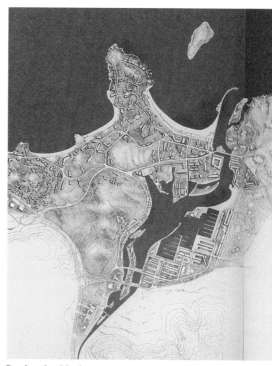

Sa Riera Park, Palma de Mallorca, by Manuel Ribas Piera, 2003-2007.

Design for Marina de Calvia by Rosa Barba, 1988.

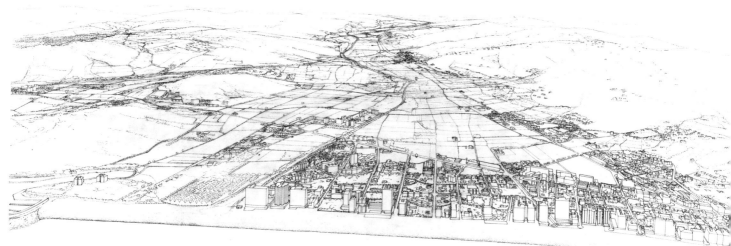

Perspective of the design for Platja d'Aro by Rosa Barba, 1981-1985.

Botanical Garden designed by Bet Figueras and Carlos Ferrater, 1999. Photo Aleix Bagué.

Elías Torres Tur, 'Y el resto...
de' in *Arquitecturas bis: infor-*
ción gráfica de actualidad, N°
29, 1979 pp. 44-50.

Nicolas M Rubió i Tudurí, *Del*
aíso al jardín latino [From
adise to the Latin garden],
81.

While it would seem almost impossible to write about pioneers
in a country where a whole generation deserves this title, at the
same time landscape architecture is still not a recognized profession in Spain and until recently it was not accepted as a separate
academic discipline with its own curriculum. Furthermore, Catalonia is a country with a singular tectonic idiosyncrasy, which has
been recycled as an exportable brand, where architecture is the
dominant design paradigm. Within this context this essay focuses
on the theme of pioneers, briefly reviewing the contribution of
three leading figures in the Barcelona landscape discipline who
went further than their colleagues and were closely involved in
the establishment of the landscape as a discipline.

HISTORY OF GARDENS RELEVANT TO PLANNERS. Manuel Ribas
Piera (born 1925) is undoubtedly one of the most influential per-
sonalities who have contributed to the foundation of landscape
architecture in Catalonia. Recognizing the academic and professional potential of the discipline already in the early 1970s, he
founded the Master´s programme in Landscape Architecture in
1983 which integrated two apparently distant collectives dedicated to the design of outdoor space in Catalonia: on one hand
there were well established professionals – gardeners and agron-
omists in the private domain of landscaping – who contributed
their experience of an expanding profession, while at the same
time he invited interested young professionals involved in the
design and reconstruction of public space in Barcelona.

The first professor to teach a course on gardens as the constant
factor in landscape making in the Urban Design and Planning
PhD programme, Manuel Ribas, traces a line that started from
the early 20th century planner Nicolau Maria Rubió i Tudurí
(a landscape designer, disciple of Forestier, hunter and writer)
whose designs, still present in the city, reflect the permanent
dilemma of Mediterranean landscape architecture[2]: that of the
attraction to European landscape styles offset against their ad-
aptation to the Mediterranean context. Manuel Ribas, still active
today, distinguished himself on this topic, designing parks and
revising relevant planning legislation, and defended emotion as
an integral part of how professional work should be received. A
cosmopolitan, yet devoted to Catalan identity, he was also the
first to travel to attend ECLAS conferences and meet landscape
professors around Europe. He is without doubt the southern representative of a generation born in the 1920s and early 1930s
that introduced landscape curricula into academia; a visionary
who in his valedictory lecture concluded that Landscape Architecture is the Urbanism of the future.

FROM TOURISM TO LANDSCAPE. One could say that coming
from a different perspective, that of planning and tourism, Rosa
Barba Casanovas (1948-2000) regarded landscape as a dis-

cipline able to provide the tools for several design issues that the physical planning of the 1970s and 80s could not resolve, oriented as it was towards infrastructure and growth. During the faltering start of landscape as a field of reflective practice, and swimming against the current, Rosa Barba Casanovas argued with conviction that professionals urgently needed training, and not only for the creation of public space. They also needed preparation to be able to deal with topics such as the sustainable development of rural areas in the process of transformation, the improvement and innovative redevelopment of established tourist destinations, and the rethinking of urban peripheries from a landscape perspective. Rosa Barba's explicit energy and critical spirit deserve mention, as they characterize her research projects on cultural landscapes and their preservation through tourist development. When introduced, this was an innovative approach; now it is one that is still present on the European research agenda.

Rosa Barba's most specific contribution, however, was the promotion of three different though complementary objectives: development of specific, applied research that would provide design topics for postgraduate courses and innovative knowhow for local administrations in relation to specific landscape demands, the introduction of landscape architecture as innovative forms of academic curricula at all education levels (being the definitive step towards establishing the landscape profession in Spain), and finally, contact with professionals elsewhere in Europe. She was a catalyst for the organization of the 1st European Biennial of Landscape Architecture, celebrated in 1999 in Barcelona with the support of the College of Architects and the Polytechnic. The huge success of the Biennial, in which over 1000 projects from all over Europe have been represented, has proved her intuition to be correct that a platform for networking and promotion of the profession was an urgent necessity.

MEDIATING BETWEEN DISCIPLINES. Last but not least, Bet Figueras Ponsa (1957-2010) represented the Spanish landscape architecture profession in a unique way from the early 1980s on. Associated with various architectural practices at the start of her career, she participated in major design projects related to the Olympics (Villa Olímpica gardens). She maintained contact with private practice during the years that she worked in the public sector, for example for the Public Space Department of the Commonwealth of Municipalities of Barcelona Region (MMAMB) or Barcelona Regional. During this period she dealt with key issues concerning the design of the city, contributing thus to the evolution of urban and public space design discourse in relation to environment and landscape.

Looking back at her early works and writings, one can see that she had already defined a precise profile for a landscape architect: neither a gardener nor an agronomist, neither an artist nor an architect. Bet Figueras always manifested how much she was learning through her exquisite collaborations and she defended elegantly landscape's professional specificity with her own work while her practice was growing from small private assignments to ones that meant involvement in outstanding public works, such as the design of the public space of the Illa Diagonal mall or the experimental botanical garden above a dump space in the Montjuic hill. She never felt that the small-scale expression of the profession was less valuable. At the same time she fought for a public representation of practitioners through her involvement in the Spanish Association of Landscape Architects. Her passion for roses, which was regarded as an extravagance at the beginning of her career, later became evidence of her wide knowledge of the basis of the profession: living design material – vegetation. In fact, her defence of the values of the Mediterranean garden was yet more proof of her commitment to contemporary inter-pretations of historical and natural processes. She always spoke about the Mediterranean garden as an expression of continuity of the surrounding landscape, not only related to identity and representation, but also as the only feasible environment in terms of construction and maintenance of landscape. Looking at Bet Figueras' professional evolution I believe that it mirrors the evolution of the landscape profession in Spain. Her work helps us experience the reinforcement and expansion of landscape architecture: its clear shift from a sophisticated though marginal design paradigm related to private initiatives and small-scale projects, to a discipline that reshapes environmental protocols and participates in the debate of the design of open space in all scales and contexts.

In a society where design is identified with architecture, Manuel Ribas, Rosa Barba, and Bet Figueras, each in their own way, fol-lowed an early intuitive understanding of the relevance of land-scape as a radical paradigm that contributes to the change of conventional design and planning attitudes, functioning as a kind of revisited humanism for an ethical future. Moreover, they are committed to its specificity, academic independence and a need for professionalism, and have worked hard to bring landscape ar-chitecture to another level, that of a hybrid design-oriented disci-pline able to improve common professional protocols. Finally, all three share their strong attraction to Europe and the belief that we belong to a bigger context and that we have to learn from each other. Their strong sense of locality was perfectly combined with an important task: to become ambassadors of the Catalo-nian landscape movement to Europe and the world, while at the same time defending the European dimension of the profession in Catalonia.

Maria Goula is Vice Dean of Landscape Studies at the School of Architecture of Barcelona and teaches Landscape Design and Landscape Theory in the Master's Programme of Landscape Architecture, ETSAB, UPC.

The roof garden highlights the artificiality of the ground. Photo Giulia Manenti

MIMOSA COURTYARD

designed by Bet Figueras landscape architect

This project updates the traditional Mediterranean garden in the middle of the dense city, namely in the interior of an *Ensanche* block. This courtyard is situated on a concrete cover, on top of the lobby of a hotel, which meant heavy structural limitations and the need to integrate the central skylights. Landscape architect Bet Figueras decided to highlight the artificiality of the ground by formulating it as a tiled floor with a special texture: taking the 2x1 proportions of the traditional *rasillas*, used in *Ensanche* patios, Figueras developed a new contemporary tile type with a special colour palette. Accordingly, contemporary clay pots refer to traditional Mediterranean planters. Mimosa is the main tree species. The interior of this city block epitomizes impressively the magic of the wider Mediterranean landscape: city and surroundings are experienced as being part of the same Mediterranean universe. [ld]

Programme Courtyard of a hotel **Designer** Bet Figueras landscape architect **In collaboration with** Carlos Ferrater, Juan Trias de Bes (architects), Patricia Urquiola (interior) **Commissioned by** Reig Capital **Area** 0.13 ha **Design** 2006–2008 **Implementation** 2009 **Budget** not applicable

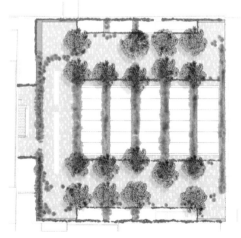

Ground plan.

PRIVATE GARDEN

designed by Bet Figueras landscape architect

The water basin 'negotiates' between two landscapes: the mountains with their Mediterranean forests and the immense sea. Photos Stefania Sabatini

This garden project evolves on a steep plot a hundred metres above sea level on the Costa Brava, at the edge of Las Gavarres mountains. Here, two landscapes meet: the mountains with their Mediterranean forests and the sea with its immense expanse of a water surface. The main feature that 'negotiates' between the two landscapes is the garden's water basin. The jury is fascinated by the refined play of contrasts in this project. It expresses the landscape architect's love for the traditional Mediterranean garden, which is an essential source of inspiration for today's cultivated landscapes in this particular region of Europe: soft vs hard materials, light vs shade, introverted vs extroverted spaces, controlled and elegant vegetation vs rustic thicket. [ld]

Programme Private house garden **Designer** Bet Figueras landscape architect **In collaboration with** TenaLorenzo Arquitectes, Ferruz Decoradors (interior) **Commissioned by** Private client **Area** 0.18 ha **Design** 2006 **Implementation** 2007–2008 **Budget** not applicable

The design expresses the landscape architect's love for the traditional Mediterranean garden.

Design.

COPENHAGEN

SENSUOUS URBANITY

Birch trees along the facade of the SEB office.

THE CITY DUNE

designed by SLA

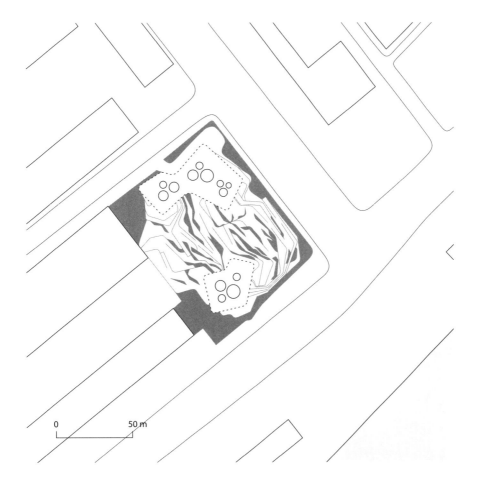

0   50 m

JURY COMMENT At first glance The City Dune provokes a hesitant response: it seems exaggerated, as it 'falls' right on top of the crossroads. Closer study removes the doubts: this project is an intriguing sign of change in an urban monoculture of offices and roads. The City Dune is a public space that is both very hard and very green at the same time. It combines the uses and functions required in a dense office area with inspiration from natural processes and ambiances. Installed on privately owned ground but allowing public access, the project provides a range of subtle sensorial experiences, and it kick-starts the development of a series of new open urban spaces on a raised level that will revitalize the whole urban transformation area in the close future. The designers offer a generous and clever urban gesture – on the one hand strategic, with greater meaning for the city, and tangible on the other, an environment that can be part of people's everyday life.

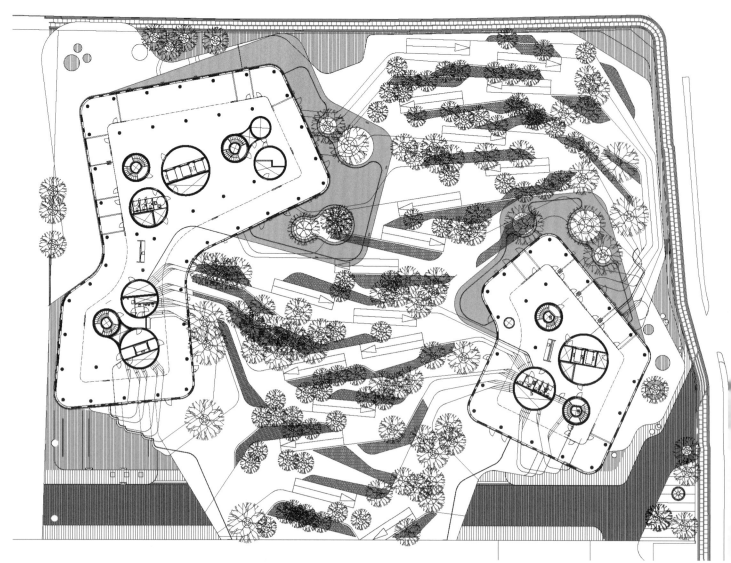

Ground plan.

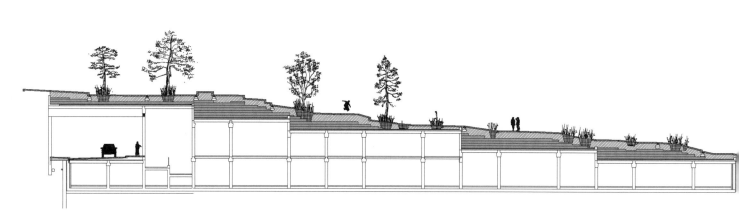

The City Dune is above a car park.

Public access and atmospheres

Feature by Mark Hendriks

The City Dune, in the old harbour area of Copenhagen, is more than just readjusted open urban space. It is a newly designed environment with an ambiance that contrasts starkly with that of the rest of this neglected part of the Danish capital. The project consists of the design of the outdoor space surrounding two new office towers that house the international SEB bank. The folded surface of The City Dune, which lies above an underground car park, is located at the busy crossroads of Kalvebod Brygge and Bernstorffsgade, where every day thousands of cars roar past anonymous hotels and offices. A path zigzags up from the street over the undulating slope. About half way up, the sounds of the cars and the city fade and the view over the centre of Copenhagen in the distance is enlivened by the foliage of beech and birch trees. Hidden nebulizers spread a cool mist – helping visitors to forget for a moment that they are in a busy city.

The morphology of The City Dune is inspired by the form and texture of the sand dunes on the north coast of Denmark – and by the pattern that is created when snow drifts settle between buildings and trees. The designers of the seven-metre high urban dune started by making a detailed analysis of natural dunes. A dune is built up as follows: the slope most affected by the wind is gentle, while the leeward side is steeper. And the same is true for The City Dune: from the windy Bernstorffsgade the dune rises gradually, while the slope on the Kalvebod Brygge side is short and steep – and at the top there is a view over the harbour and residential tower blocks in Amagerbro on the other side of the water. The analogy goes further. An important characteristic of sand dunes is that they drift; especially areas that have no plants anchoring them. In the coastal areas, patches of drifting sand – before they became grown over – had a large influence on the topog-

Cross section.

raphy for many centuries. 'Encroaching' dunes covered vegetation and inundated houses. The artificial dune in the old harbour of Copenhagen behaves in the same way. The white concrete of The City Dune appears to form mounds between the two office towers, just like sand or snow. What's more: this pattern continues in the glass facades of the lobbies to the bank buildings.

The sand dune metaphor doesn't mean, however, that the SLA landscape architects office have imitated a natural and lush dune area around the bank buildings in Copenhagen. On the contrary: the intention was to create a pleasant and accessible, but above all urban space – in which the analysis of the North Danish sand dune landscape served merely as an inspiration. This is visible in the multitude of artificial interventions that have to do with sustainability and climate control. For example, the white concrete surface reflects a great deal of heat from the sun, without detracting from the strength of the sunrays. As a result, the temperature on The City Dune remains pleasant on hot summer days. The mist from the artificial nebulizers – which spring into life randomly day and night – provides cooling. They use rainwater that has been collected and recycled, as do the trees that have been planted in the area: birch, beech, pine and other conifers. The water that is collected is also used to water the plants and grasses in the borders. Not a drop finds its way into the city sewers.

The most salient reference to a natural system is the expression of capriciousness in the urban space. No two visits will be the same, for each depends on the moment in time, the weather, the light or the visitor's mood. Wandering through the area, The City Dune has a different feel depending on whether it is evening or daytime; summer or autumn; and whether it is rainy or the sun is shining. Apart from this, it is evidenced in the programme of requirements upon which the plan is based that The City Dune is a totally planned and designed urban space, and therefore not a natural environment that has grown spontaneously. The boundaries, the routing, the way in which the white concrete 'clothes' the car park roof – all stem from functional and technical conditions stipulating accessibility for the elderly and wheelchair users, drainage, planting requirements, illumination and use. The design and construction language is strong, but understated: stepped areas, mechanical nebulizers, circular planting holes in the concrete for the trees, the advanced lighting system and the multiform borders.

The project is part of a large-scale development in which, under the supervision of SLA, the dilapi-

dated harbour area will bring new value to the city. The idea is to create a seven-metre tall 'high line' above multi-storey car parks and across new building complexes, which connects the old city centre with a railway station on adjacent derelict harbour sites. The City Dune is the first step: on the city side the artificial dune forms the entrance to the raised walk and cycle route. This is possible because the owner, SEB, is obliged under Danish law to keep the space open to the public. It will take a while before The City Dune can actually live up to its role as the connector between city and harbour – the two following complexes have been built and the others are right now in the planning phase.

Programme Design of a privately owned space for the public in a central harbour and railway transformation area **Designer** SLA **In collaboration with** Lundgaard & Tranberg Arkitekter (building), Rambøll A/S (construction) **Commissioned by** SEB Bank & Pension **Area** 0.73 ha **Design** 2005–2007 **Implementation** 2007–2010 **Budget** € 4,700,000

The terrain was previously used as a car park.

e City Dune forms a mound between the new SEB offices. Photo Jens Lindhe

the summer nebulizers provide an occasional cooling mist.

At the Kalvebod Brygge the slope is steeper. Above is the entrance to one of the two office towers of SEB.

The City Dune design is based on the sand dunes along the north coast of Denmark. Photo Jens Lindhe

From the Bernstorffsgade the white concrete of The City Dune gradually rises.

rch and pine trees have been planted randomly.

The design and construction language is hard and green as well.

Skaters enjoy the height differences.

IN BETWEEN – DANISH LANDSCAPE LINEAGES

Essay by Mads Farsø

In comparison with many other European countries, landscape architecture is relatively widely recognized in Denmark and the landscape profession enjoys a corresponding position of strength. It is thus taken for granted that landscape architects should be involved in all larger construction projects and that landscape architecture is also discussed outside the specialized professional media. This relatively strong position is interpreted as being a result of a historical development, in which both structural circumstances and influential individuals have played a part.

After the First World War the Danish social housing corporations grew strong and became instrumental in the supply of housing. The late 1930s were the golden age of the social housing movement in Denmark, when many of the country's best architects took part in the development of the new social housing projects – and it was not only architects who were engaged on these projects; landscape architects were also involved as a matter of course. Although the profession at this time did not have many practitioners, it included some very talented and strong individuals. The publication in 1930 of the treatise *Der kommende Garten* (The Garden of the Future) by Gudmund Nyeland Brandt (1878-1945) was a landmark for Danish garden art. In this Brandt set out his ideas for a garden reflecting the modern cultural landscape, which – as opposed to an architectural or geometric garden – formalized cultural landscape features by referring to hedgerows, commons or groves. The treatise addressed the predominance of the landscape in the garden concept and it led to an implicit upgrading of the garden architect to landscape architect, both in terms of professional recognition and scale of projects. Brandt, a gardener who had also taken classes in philosophy, became the first lecturer in garden art at the Royal Danish Academy of Fine Arts, School of Architecture (1924-41). He inspired a new generation of landscape architects and opened the way for one of his students, C.Th. Sørensen (1893-1979), to become professor at the School of Architecture. In 1946 the professor of garden art at the Royal Veterinary and Agricultural School, Georg Georgsen (1893-1873), proposed that landscape architecture should be taught separately.

The social housing movement was from the start very ambitious with regard to creating new housing developments and whole urban quarters that would demonstrate how a healthy and aesthetically pleasing working class neighbourhood could be shaped and delivered. Landscape architecture came to play an important part in the social housing corporations' work at an early stage, because it responded to the health agenda and the desire to provide good recreational areas, but also because landscape architects like Brandt and later Sørensen understood how to both promote and deliver solutions that were immediately convincing and worked in relation to the existing social and economic context.

It was after the Second World War in particular that the profession expanded quantitatively. New teaching positions were established in landscape architecture, and the profession expanded in step with the explosive building and construction activity that followed the establishment of the welfare state and the general economic growth in the post-war period. In 1960 a new landscape course was established under the gardener programme at the Royal Veterinary and Agricultural School, now Copenhagen University, where Georg Boye (1906-1072), who had worked at Sørensen's office, became professor. Sven Hansen (1910-1989), who had worked at Brandt's office, became one of the first teachers in landscape architecture at the School of Architecture in Århus and later professor (1976-1980). The division of work and the perception among landscape architects dictated that the landscape architect developed the open spaces that the architects' and town planners' building plans had defined – and the planners and architects concurred in this view. This understanding of the profession's position was challenged and overridden, however, in some of Sørensen's projects with larger parks, as well as his participation in the development of building plans and alignment of motorways – in the same way one could increasingly see landscape architects in the other Scandinavian countries and in Germany taking on a leading role in the shaping of large-scale plans. Other Danish representatives of such trends were the landscape architects Aksel Andersen (1903-52), Georg Boye (1906-1972), Edith and Ole Nørgård (1919-89 and 1925-78), Agnete Muusfeldt (1918-91) and Jørn Palle Schmidt (1923-2010).

The Swede Sven-Ingvar Andersson (1927-2007) can be regarded as an exponent of a generation of landscape architects and landscape architecture that began to demand another, more prominent and independent role in the division of work between town planners, architects and landscape architects. Like Brandt, Andersson had a diverse professional background. He was educated as an art historian, gardener and landscape architect and therefore had a variety of approaches to the profession. The expansion and consolidation of the welfare state lead to growing construction capacity and resulted in still more new projects for landscape architects on the domestic scene. While Andersson found his place in the professional context in Denmark, there were also new opportunities for landscape architecture in many

Th. Sørensen, Højstrup Park, 1948. Buildings frame **plot and allow for the creation of a central park.** rce: C.Th. Sørensen. A Landscape Modernist. The Danish Archi-ural Press, 2001

G. N. Brandt, Mariebjerg cemetery, 1926. Trees are linkages. Photo: Mads Farsø

Nørgård-Harboe-Ginmann, Kongsholmparken, 1969. Plantings emphasize the hill.
Source: ARKITEKTUR DK 4/ 1990

n Hansen, Gardens of Glostrup Hospital, 1952. Field- **nes refer to the Danish Ice Age landscape.** rce. ARKITEKTUR DK 4/ 1990

Steen Høyer, town development scheme for Aalborg, 1998. Landscape and city integrated.
Source: Steen Høyer. Landskabskunst. Kunstakademiets Arkitekt-skoles Forlag, 2006

en-Ingvar Andersson, sketch for Parc de la Villette competition entry, 1982. Source: Landskab 3/ 1983

other countries that inspired him to take part in even more types of projects and competitions. He took part successfully, for example, in the Parc de la Villette competition. The larger 'volume' of the profession provided the landscape architects with potential, power and self-confidence to participate in large international competitions.

Sven-Ingvar Andersson's department at the School of Architecture and his practice in Copenhagen became a laboratory where new projects and new approaches to the subject were tested and practised. Inspiring and creative environments grew around Andersson, which attracted young, talented people and prompted them to establish their own practices. His employee Steen Høyer (born 1945) was later appointed to continue his professorship the School of Architecture, while Stig Lennart Andersson (born 1957), who worked at Andersson's practice for a short period, was recently appointed professor of the landscape architecture programme at the University of Copenhagen, into which the former Royal Veterinary and Agricultural School has been integrated.

Today the practice of the profession has broadened to include an increasing role within town planning and other large-scale planning projects, and a new and more self-assured approach to smaller projects, where the landscape architect's work often contributes to defining the principal identity of a new development – as recently exemplified by Stig Lennart Andersson's project *The City Dune* for the SEB Bank in Copenhagen, one of the features in this book. There are parts of this re-alignment that are related to structural conditions such as EU tendering processes – and there are parts that can be explained as being parallel to international developments – but there is still a large part that must be assigned the specific historical context and the prominent individuals that have influenced the Danish landscape scene.

In this sense, *The City Dune* could perhaps be viewed as an alternative version of Brandt's idea of design, because the design project could be referenced to the experience of a landscape – such as a hike in the rocky parts of Sweden, which is the place of origin of the SEB bank, or a climb on the voluminous fortifications of Copenhagen that used to be in the nearby area. In this city, mostly defined by globalized capital and by works of architecture, it represents landscape architecture introduced as an identity-generating element, a manifestation of landscape, the in-between being the key element.

Mads Farsø is a PhD fellow, teacher and landscape architect at the Department of Geoscience, Natural Resources and Planning, University of Copenhagen. The essay was developed in dialogue with Jens Kvorning, Professor and Head of the Centre for Urban Planning (Department 1 City and Landscape), School of Architecture, The Royal

LANDSCAPE POLICIES

DRENTHE

The *strubben* are being cleared of excess vegetation.
Previous pages: The diffuse pattern of the *strubben*, between the forest and heather areas, is visible from the air. On the south and east side, the straight edge of the old Kniphorst estate forest can be seen. All photos (except above) Harry Cock

STRUBBEN KNIPHORSTBOSCH

designed by Strootman Landschapsarchitecten

0   500 m

JURY COMMENT This development and management plan can be seen as a progressive strategy to conserve, develop and manage cultural heritage within the natural surroundings of the Strubben Kniphorstbosch area. The designers succeed in enhancing the readability and the spatial coherence of the area, and they deliver one possible answer to the question of how to provide space for both cultural history and nature development, while preparing the landscape for future developments. Still one question arises: doesn't this landscape design, in which the official goals of nature preservation have been subordinated to those of cultural history, tend towards a reconstruction of a landscape of former times?

Late Neolithic burial mound, E
and Middle Bronze Age

burial mound in Late Bronze A
Early Iron Age

tumulus in the Late Iron Age

Middle Neolithic megalith grave

possible traces of Celtic field

distinct cart tracks

heathland

ridge

grassland with scarce heathlar

shifting sand area

heathland with depression

small pool / hollow

field / meadow

holt / wood

old forest

oak shrub vegetation

forest with outdoor character

seedbed forest

production forest

transparent production forest

spontaneous forest

avenue and wooded bank

oaks placed out of line

parking area

visual relationship with environ

former shooting range and ass
course

(Bailey)bridge or underpass N3
in the direction of Annen

solitary tree

Development and management plan. On the old estate the structure of the avenues and several sightlines have been restored. In the southern part of the Strubben Kniphorstbosch trees and shrubs have been cut down to reveal the longitudinal cart tracks.

The development of the 'green' blanket over the years – as a result of which the relationship between and the visibility of historical remains has disappeared.

Dramatizing the differences between nature and culture

Feature by Mark Hendriks

The Strubben Kniphorstbosch nature reserve in the Drentsche Aa catchment area is the biggest national archaeological monument in the Netherlands. In the area between Anloo, Annen and Schipborg countless remains of human habitation spanning thousands of years can be found. The landscape on top of and around De Hondsrug, a seventy-kilometre-long sand ridge – of which the Strubben Kniphorstbosch is part – was one of the liveliest and most densely populated regions of the lowlands from prehistoric times until the Middle Ages.

Encompassing nearly 300 hectares, the area is home to burial mounds, megalithic *hunebeds* and Celtic fields (ancient fields in a patchwork quilt pattern) from the Neolithic, Bronze and Iron Age. There are also remains of deep litter housing and heather grazing, fence posts and medieval cart tracks – an important trade route from Groningen to Coevorden ran through the area at the time. In the central part, elements are still present of the nineteenth-century Kniphorst estate, such as avenues and blocks of densely planted trees, and the area is littered with objects from the period when Strubben Kniphorstbosch was used as a military training ground.

When the area came under ownership of the nature conservation organization Staatsbosbeheer in 2006, the features of archaeological and historical value were almost invisible. For decades the Strubben Kniphorstbosch had been maintained as an 'ordinary' area of nature and woodland, not only by the Ministry of Defence, but also by Staatsbosbeheer itself. During this period nature was to take its course and much of the historical and archaeological remains had become overgrown by a 'green blanket' of woodland. The historical remains had become unrecognizable and the area lacked coherence. Staatsbosbeheer commissioned a landscape and management plan from the Amsterdam-based Strootman Landschapsarchitecten that – while taking into account natural and landscape features – would bring renewed attention to the historical importance of the Strubben Kniphorstbosch.

The designers have adopted an approach whereby a new and 'staged' landscape will be created within ten years. Using subtle and, at times, stronger design and management interventions, the cohesion between the historical and archaeological monuments is made more visible. The idea is to create a landscape where visitors can experience historical features without having to resort to aids such as information boards.

For Staatsbosbeheer as the commissioning body, this landscape architectonic approach represents a break with a management approach in which biodiversity and achieving nature conservation and recreational targets have traditionally been the prime focus. In the design and management of the Strubben Kniphorstbosch, 'nature objectives' have become subordinate to the creation of a clear landscape that is full of contrast and where the historical stratification can be re-experienced. This has repercussions for the way in which Staatsbosbeheer will undertake long-term maintenance of the Strubben Kniphorstbosch. Sheep will be allowed to graze once again in the open areas to keep them free of encroaching vegetation. The shepherds, foresters and other maintenance workers will work in a way that is no longer species and ecosystem oriented, but directed at maintaining the designed landscape.

The focus is on the restoration of the contrast between the 'uncultivated grounds' of heather fields and shifting sands in the north and south, and the 'cultivated grounds' of the rational woodland and estate landscape in the centre.

The measures have already been implemented in the northern part. The heather landscape with cart tracks, burial mounds and *strubben* has been cleared of excess vegetation. *Strubben* are low oak shrubs that grew among the heather from the fifteenth century and were prevented from growing larger by grazing sheep. As the flocks of sheep disappeared in the nineteenth century with the arrival of artificial fertilizer, oak and beech trees gradually outgrew the *strubben*. By felling the surrounding trees, the *strubben* once again retain prominence in the landscape. The diffuse pattern that they form creates a spatial transition between the dense old forest on the north-western edge and the open heather to the south. In the same north-western corner, the excess vegetation around a parabolic dune formed during the ice age has also been cleared. Among the freestanding *strubben* the Iron Age burial mounds have once again become visible. On the southern side of the heather, De Galgenberg – a burial mound upon which a gallows was erected at a later date – has been designed as a landmark with an attractive view of the surrounding area. The open heather field ('uncultivated land') contrasts with the closed, rectilinear production forest of conifers on the former Kniphorst estate ('cultivated grounds'). This is emphasized by long, straight edges to the forests.

The Strubben Kniphorstbosch landscape and management plan was elaborated from the landscape vision that Strootman Landschapsarchitecten designed in 2005 for the Drentsche Aa catchment area, which was included in the previous Yearbook *On Site*. The landscape vision is a strategy that articulates the landscape in its ecological and historical diversity. It offers a framework which can be used to consider the effects of political choices on all scales. It shows how the landscape of the Drentsche Aa will develop depending on whether one opts for agriculture, for nature, for recreation or for heritage.

In the Strubben Kniphorstbosch the choice is clear: the traces of archaeological and historical heritage receive priority, in principle. In a valuable area of nature like the Strubben Kniphorstbosch, however, a change of direction like this has not been without some controversial interventions, including the felling of many trees, the creation of empty, open spaces, the retention of 'poor' conifer forest and making straight edges to forested areas. The tree felling caused the most commotion. Local residents and nature organizations presented reasons why certain trees should not be felled: one tree was above a badger sett; one was part of a tree circle believed to have spiritual powers; and another tree was of great value to nearby residents, and so on. As a result, 'on-the-spot' adjustments were made to the plan: on location and sometimes actually during the felling activities. Nevertheless, the design of the landscape was always kept in mind. This way of working is reminiscent of the eighteenth-century English landscape architect and gardener Lancelot 'Capability' Brown: the designer only arrives at the right composition once in the field.
The question arises whether this focus on cultural heritage would have been tenable if the Strubben Kniphorstbosch had been of outstanding ecological value. The felling and thinning of young growth is not harmful in ecological terms because rare animal and plant species in the area benefit from more openness. Furthermore the conserved *strubben* form part of the European Natura 2000 nature network, and the straight forest edges – which appear to be in contradiction with the principles of nature development – actually offer opportunities for new species, such as blueberries, butterflies and adders.

The approach adopted in the Strubben Kniphorstbosch must be considered within the context of contemporary political shifts concerning nature and cultural heritage. Until recently, much effort was devoted to strengthening the position of cultural heritage in regional development and landscape planning in the Netherlands, under the Belvedere programme. Unlike the Dutch monument policy, this was not so much about protecting heritage, but about 'conservation through development': historical features would gain a new meaning and thus be secured for the future. Nature policy on the other hand has come increasingly under fire. In the Netherlands, nature management is being regarded more and more as an activity of the elite: it is seen as being solely concerned with the conservation of rare plant and animal species and too far removed from the reality of 'the people'.

These tendencies come together in the Strubben Kniphorstbosch. When it comes to the 'conservation through development' ideology, this project tends towards 'museumization' of a landscape of former times. On the other hand, conservation of species and biotopes is not the only focus, rather it is about the development of an accessible and understandable landscape – where visitors are overwhelmed by the immense number of historical monuments. Regarding the political claim that nature and landscape management is a one-sided and elitist affair, the Strubben Kniphorstbosch project is proof that the opposite is the case.

Programme Development and management plan for a nature reserve and archaeological monument **Designer** Strootman Landschapsarchitecten **In collaboration with** NovioConsult, Bureau Overland, University of Groningen (Centre for Landscape Studies) **Commissioned by** Staatsbosbeheer, Dutch nature conservation organization (with financial support from The Netherlands Architecture Fund) **Area** 295 ha **Design** 2007–2008 **Implementation** 2009–2019 (the northern part was realized in 2011) **Budget** € 1,060,000

| conversion of spontaneous woodland to grazed open heath with a few solitary trees | clearing of cart tracks = removal of deposits and undergrowth to make cart tracks visible | | thinning out of oaks along former marken boundary | possible creation of a new tidy border of Norway spruce in the long term |

spontaneous wood with Scots pine, ordinary broad-leaved trees and undergrowth   concealed cart tracks and sand ridges   concealed cart tracks and sand ridges   former *marke* boundary   production wood with conifers

Present situation

inside outside
grazing area

open heath with a few solitary trees   visible cart tracks and sand ridges   visible cart tracks and sand ridges   views towards Strubbenvelds   exeptional oak trees   new tidy fringe visible from open heath

Future situation

15 m

The Strubben area on the plateau of Schipborg

Reclaimed area (commercial forests and Kniphorstbosch)

Aeolian sands and heath-land area with the sandy depressions Berekuil [bear-pit] and Jerusalem

[la]yout of the landscape [uni]ts.

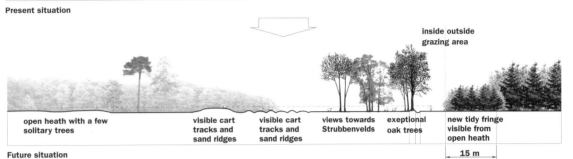

Transect and impression of the interventions around the parabolic dune in the northern part.

- axis hollow
- ridge
- peat depression (hollow with a surrounding bank)
- plateaus at Schipborg / at Anloo
- urnfields / remaining urnfields
- settlement site
- Late Neolithic burial mound, Early and Middle Bronze Age
- burial mound in Late Bronze Age Early Iron Age
- tumulus in the Late Iron Age
- Middle Neolithic megalith grave
- possible traces of Celtic field
- holt / wood
- oak shrub vegetation
- parking area
- cart tracks / distinct
- cart tracks / vague

- open places in the forest at present
- future open places in the forest
- future transparent forest
- future forested areas
- field / meadow

[m]ap of all historical features and finds.

The crux of the design: increasing the contrast between open and closed spaces.

Before and after: by cutting down excess trees (above) a clear landscape has been created (right).

o historical features: a burial mound and a bomb crater.

Sheep graze on the heather again.

THE POWER OF THE EUROPEAN LANDSCAPE CONVENTION

Essay by Ingrid Sarlöv Herlin

Policies shape landscapes. As we observe in the Dutch *Strubben Kniphorstbosch* project, a changing understanding of landscape and heritage values has been translated into regional and national policies, which in turn have provided the conceptual basis for the landscape architects' design. These translation processes – of societal values into legislative frameworks – are often overlooked by the design profession, as they lie far from their core business, are taken for granted or seem out of reach. However, their influence is direct and no landscape design will ever develop beyond the opportunities offered by legislation. This is the reason why, on a European level, an initiative emerged to draw up a codex that would translate the values that the landscape architecture profession attributes to contemporary landscapes, and to propose that this document represent a common horizon of understanding for landscapes and their development across Europe. The initiative has been successful: the document, named the European Landscape Convention (ELC), has been produced and is now being promoted at the political levels that are able to influence legislative powers. This is an ambitious project, and yet it is striking how many of Europe's designers still ignore its nature, its scope and its work modes – the power of the ELC lies in engagement!

The ELC is the first international treaty that addresses landscapes. Known also as the Florence Convention, it is just over a decade old, having been adopted in October 2000, in Florence, Italy. Today 35 of Council of Europe's 47 member states have signed and ratified the ELC, which means that in principle they have approved the convention. A further four states have signed it only, without further ratification. The reputation of the ELC has spread during its short lifespan, and today most people dealing with landscape are aware of the existence of the convention. There are, however, two frequently occurring misunderstandings of the concepts upon which it is based.

WHAT THE ELC IS NOT. The first misunderstanding is that the ELC has something to do with the European Union. This is not the case. The ELC is a convention developed by the Council of Europe in Strasbourg, an intergovernmental organization that was created after the Second World War to promote human rights, democracy and right of law in Europe. The ELC is closely related to the range of other international legal instruments, such as the Unesco Convention concerning the Protection of the World Cultural and Natural Heritage (Paris 1972); the Council of Europe Convention on the Conservation of European Wildlife and Natural Habitats (Bern 1979); the Council of Europe Convention for the Protection of the Architectural Heritage of Europe (Granada, 1985); and the Council of Europe Convention for the Protection of the Archaeological Heritage (Valletta, 1992).

The second misinterpretation is that the ELC might have direct legal implications at the European level, as for example an EU-directive or a law does. This is not the case either. It is 'nothing more' than a convention, an agreement between states, thus not legally binding. States that have signed and ratified the ELC but do not follow it cannot be prosecuted for this. If states fail in their commitment to the convention they are likely to be regarded as failing in their obligations and are hence likely to be 'ostracized'. Each country that ratifies the ELC has 'to recognise landscapes in law as an essential component of people's surroundings, an expression of the diversity of their shared cultural and natural heritage, and a foundation of their identity'. The legal implications of the ELC therefore manifest themselves at the national level, not the European.

WHAT THE ELC IS. The ELC is the first international treaty that deals with the protection, management and planning (which in this context also includes design) of landscapes, and is intended to promote cooperation on landscape issues within Europe. One of its major objectives is to strengthen public and local community participation in decision-making related to landscape. An overall objective of the convention is to achieve sustainable development based on a 'harmonious and balanced relationship between social needs, economic activity and the environment'. The ELC is a territorial convention. This means that it covers all natural, rural, urban and peri-urban areas. It includes land, inland water and marine areas. Not only landscapes with special conservation values or outstanding landscapes are covered, but also everyday landscapes, and even landscapes that are degraded or undergoing decay. In addition, the ELC emphasizes that landscape can contribute to the formation of local cultures and that landscape is an important element of Europe's natural and cultural heritage, contributing to regional characteristics, local identity, sense of place, memories and associations, views, and the experience of nature and cultural heritage. The ELC describes how the landscape brings a range of benefits to society in the cultural, environmental and social domains. The landscape is acknowledged as contributing to people's well-being and health, as well as being a resource for recreation, tourism, economic development and ecosystem services. The protection, management and planning of landscapes contributes to job creation according to the explanatory report of the ELC. The emphasis on urban and everyday landscapes is of particular importance, as over half of the world's population now lives in cities.

rences
he full text of the Eu-
an Landscape Conven-
can be found at http://
entions.coe.int/Treaty/
mun/QueVoulezVous.
PNT=176&CM=8&CL=ENG
related convention is the
ncil of Europe Framework
vention on the Value of
ural Heritage for Society
, 2005), which can be
d at http://conventions.
int/Treaty/EN/Treaties/
/199.htm
he Council of Europe
ides information about
ng activities in the differ-
countries concerning the
pean Landscape Conven-
at: http://www.coe.int/t/
cultureheritage/heritage/
scape/default_en.asp
he autumn issue 2/2011
cape, the international
azine for landscape archi-
ure and urbanism, contains
ssier on 'power play',
ding the full length version
is essay by Ingrid Sarlöv
in on the European Land-
e Convention, complete
articles and reports on
ELC from the Netherlands,
ium, Germany, Switzerland
Spain. See www.scape-
azine.com

HOW THE ELC WORKS. Individual countries that have rati-fied the ELC have to follow a range of general and specific measures. The first is, as previously mentioned, to include 'landscape' in each country's own environmental or planning legislation. Implementation of the convention is taking place according to the prerequisites of each individual country. In the spirit of the ELC, this procedure allows for diversity between the different European countries according to their cultures and characteristics, instead of requiring standardized methods for implementation and monitoring.

The European Landscape Convention takes a holistic approach to landscape, which it defines as 'an area that is perceived by people, whose character is the result of the action and inter-action of natural and/or human factors'. This explanation is based on the notion that a 'landscape forms a whole, whose natural and cultural components are taken together, not sepa-rately'. The perception of landscape is not limited to sight only; we can experience it with all our senses: hearing, touch, smell and taste. The ELC describes landscape as dynamic by its very nature and can or should not therefore be frozen in one par-ticular state. As stated in the preamble of the ELC, the aim should rather 'be to manage future changes in a way which recognises the great diversity and the quality of the land-scapes' and 'to preserve, or even enhance, that diversity and quality instead of allowing them to decline'.

The contracting states commit themselves to identify their own landscapes; to analyse characteristics and driving forces and to monitor landscape changes. Awareness raising and interdisciplinary training and education on all levels are also highlighted. One of the most important measures proposed by the convention is to enhance local participation and participa-tory democracy in planning, management and protection of the landscape, as stated in the preamble: 'If people are given an active role in decision-making on landscape, they are more likely to identify with the areas and towns where they spend their working and leisure time. If they have more influence on their surroundings, they will be able to reinforce local and regional identity and distinctiveness and this will bring rewards in terms of individual, social and cultural fulfilment. This in turn may help to promote the sustainable development of the area.'

This emphasis on governance in decision-making regarding planning, management and protection of landscapes is chal-lenging the prevailing top-down approaches in place in most countries. The ELC has sometimes (and wrongly) been antici-pated as a tool for preventing negative landscape impacts and is therefore often welcomed by people described as 'nimbies'

(Not In My Backyard) and others who are against changes. We reiterate: the ELC cannot be of direct use as a planning tool in such a context, but it may be useful for developing landscape considerations in policy and legalization, and as a guide towards better procedures and methods involving a higher degree of public participation. The major power of the ELC lies in its ability to change ideas and perspectives among planners, designers, managers, politicians, educators, researchers, NGOs and local stakeholders.

TEST THE ELC! We need to tread carefully before pronouncing the time ripe for further promotion of the ELC as an international convention. The concept and understanding of landscape is as diverse in Europe as the European landscapes themselves, and languages and cultures outside Europe have even more divergent perspectives on the notion of landscape. In an international perspective it is important that the ELC is not pushed too precipitately in the wrong direction, the danger being the creation of an ILC (which some would term an 'Imperialistic Landscape Convention') dominated by a European paradigm on landscape. It would be sensible to explore the full potential of the ELC in Europe before extending it to a global level, so that we fully understand its pitfalls. The ELC has been created to highlight the multiple values of landscape, to encourage a more dynamic understanding of it and to foster a holistic perspective that embraces a more profound integration of natural and cultural perspectives and places the focus on people.

Dr Ingrid Sarlöv Herlin is a landscape architect and professor of landscape planning at the Department of Landscape Architecture at the Swedish University of Agricultural Sciences (SLU) in Alnarp/Malmö. She is a member of the advisory board for *Landscapes* (Windgather Press/ Oxbow Books) and of the international

LEISURE LANDSCAPES

MARGHERA

The gravel path takes up the trace of an old ditch which collects rainwater and carries it to the wetlands at the edge of the park.

CATENE PARK

designed by CZstudio associati

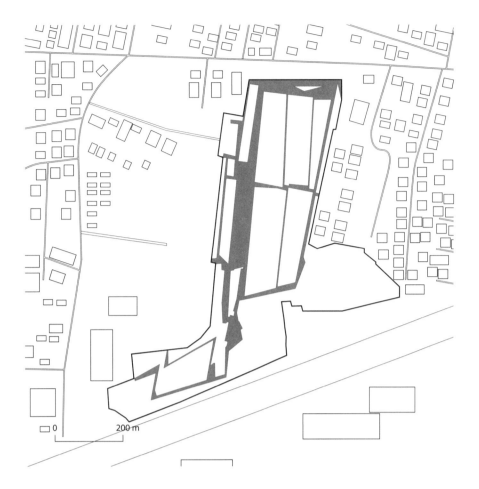

0   200 m

JURY COMMENT This project shows a sensitive approach to the transformation of former agricultural land into a contemporary urban park including sports and play, on the fringes of the city. Instead of installing a nostalgic rural imagery, the designers stick to the fundaments of the cultivated landscape: they have taken over the hydraulic structure of the former fields and renewed the materials of the urban landscape. The park is conceived as a large open expanse in the built up surroundings and it integrates spaces for specific uses into a framework composed of elegant design elements, the execution of which is of a high quality.

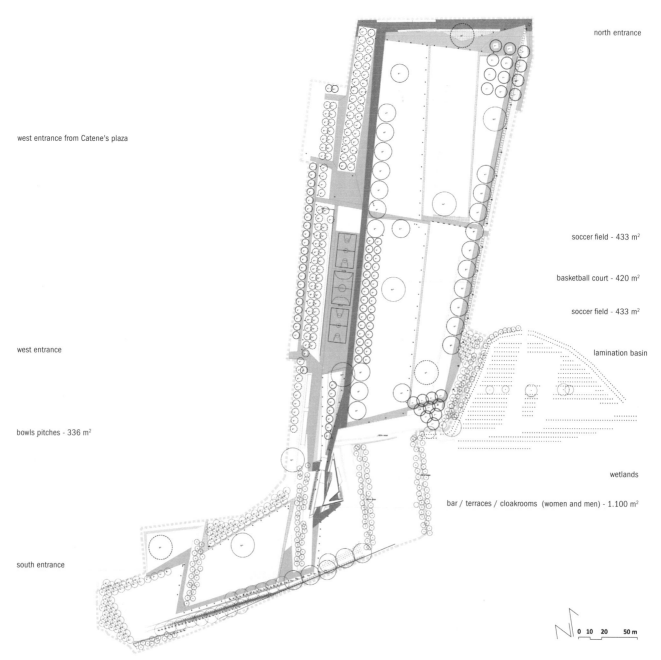

west entrance from Catene's plaza

north entrance

west entrance

soccer field - 433 m²

basketball court - 420 m²

soccer field - 433 m²

lamination basin

bowls pitches - 336 m²

wetlands

bar / terraces / cloakrooms (women and men) - 1.100 m²

south entrance

0 10 20   50 m

Transformation of agricultural land into urban park.

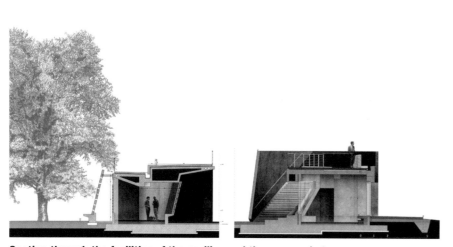

Section through the facilities of the pavilion and the panoramic terrace.

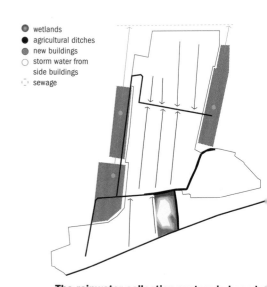

- ● wetlands
- ● agricultural ditches
- ● new buildings
- ○ storm water from side buildings
- ⬚ sewage

**The rainwater collection system is based o
pre-existing agricultural plots.**

Urban practices on agricultural land

Feature by Thierry Kandjee

The Catene Park project forms part of the overall renewal of the city of Marghera, an industrial town near Venice and Mestre. Located in a district of 6000 inhabitants that was linked with the fertilizer industry in the 1950s, the project transforms a derelict plot of land into an attractive urban facility. Situated between heavy infrastructure to the south (A4 motorway) and a transit route to the north (via Trieste) bordered here and there by new real-estate developments, the 8-hectare park offers locals and new residents a re-reading of the agricultural layout upon which the town was founded.

Crossing Marghera from south to north is a multiple learning experience. Industrial space is predominant on the fringes of the area, contiguous with the Venetian Lagoon. The city centre presents numerous traces of the town's rural heritage, with squares and neighbourhood parks, and tree lined streets Catene district consists of densely built housing on a plot of land that seems agricultural, contiguous throughout with the via Trieste. Situated between a service station and a housing development, Catene

Park suggests an uncommon meeting of conserved agricultural land with new urban uses.

The project is based on a series of clear, easily identifiable measures. In the first instance, the hydraulic structure of the site is the project's underlying element. The pre-existing agricultural ditches on the site have been redirected to gravelled paths that drain water throughout the site toward agricultural land that has now become wetlands. From the northern entry point, these large traces set out the main lines of direction of the site toward the pre-existing wooded edge and constitute its principal morphology. The conserved wetlands, which are out of bounds for pedestrians, ensure ecological sustainability and reduce the risk of flooding in this district that is subject to population densification. In addition, some of the water is stored to irrigate new areas of planting plantations. The park is a product of meticulous attention to the design of its borders in close consideration of the site's everyday uses. In direct contrast with via Trieste, whose urban vocabulary is generic, the northern border of the park negoti-

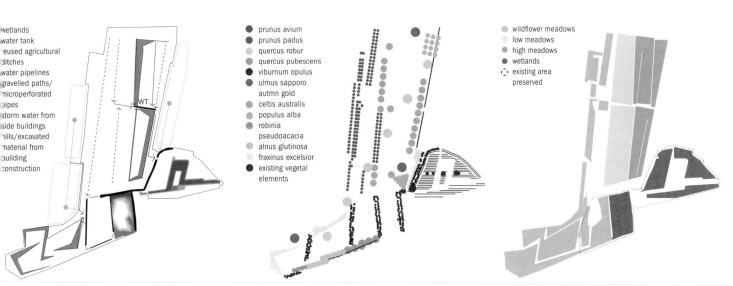

wetlands
water tank
reused agricultural
ditches
water pipelines
gravelled paths/
microperforated
pipes
storm water from
side buildings
hills/excavated
material from
building
construction

prunus avium
prunus padus
quercus robur
quercus pubescens
viburnum opulus
ulmus sapporo
autmn gold
celtis australis
populus alba
robinia
pseudoacacia
alnus glutinosa
fraxinus excelsior
existing vegetal
elements

wildflower meadows
low meadows
high meadows
wetlands
existing area
preserved

draulic system.   Tree planting.   Ground cover vegetation.

ates a carefully tended threshold and is indicative of a desire to express quality workmanship with simple materials. A wide concrete pathway accommodating a bus stop extends along the entire width of the park to the north. From the street, the long 2m-high gabion wall just about enables one to catch a glimpse of the breadth of the land and the foliage of existing trees. Past the wall, the park takes on the form of a large expanse, a wide plain composed of 4 hectares of grassland. The site reveals a view of an existing wooded area at the edges, which forms the starting point for a delicate play on the site's topology. The form of the embankments is based on the lines of the existing ditches and invites a range of perceptions. At the level of the site, the suggested reading is that of a depression and a depth which forms a setting for the installed amenities. All along the site, a concrete platform in the form of a wide bench links a series of sporting amenities and a café, multipurpose room and toilet facilities in matching materials. These amenities are simultaneously a passage, a shelter and a surface of the park. The roof slopes into two open terraces onto the overall site. This space is indicative of a strong desire to encourage a mix of uses for this open expanse, by day and by night. The multipurpose room is used by school groups and clubs. The structure has already been accepted by the local adolescents who see it as a special place. Intentionally placed at a crossroads of movement on the site, the multipurpose room has a hospitality function that goes beyond the local district.

The design of space in this park interprets agricultural know-how in terms of working on sloping ground. The play on the differences in level highlights the strata involved in the project: the low-lying existing ditches planted with high-branched trees, the new sporting areas level with the town, the main pathways done in brushed concrete; on a higher level, sloping lawns and embankments and the multipurpose room structure. The CZ studio project highlights each one of these horizons. The slope of the grasslands plays on the changing surfaces in a manner that catches the light, suggesting a long-established, comfortable setting in this park with its young plantings. The walls on the fringes add a dimension to the scenery of the site and permit a degree of emancipation from the urban context. The specific marking-out of the draining paths and more frequented areas, designed using simple elements, underlines the overall project.

To the south, the park borders the highway and engages with a supermarket built afterward. Although the junction between these two spaces may not be perfectly accomplished, the fact remains that the car park attached to this commercial area is the sole point of access to the highway leading to the southern part of the town. In this specific, diffuse territory, public parking spaces take on new urban features which are to the park's benefit. In the same way, the park opens out to lateral paths and public spaces along its fringes. It is part of a chain of open spaces extending beyond this one district. The care accorded to the connections between the park and its immediate context, while avoiding any notion of enclosure, contributes to the park's successful integration. The first impression of the park from its two points of entry is that of a landscape that is open and welcoming to urban users.

Far removed from any notion of nostalgia, the land is both reused and transformed into a park that cleverly facilitates co-existence of urban uses and ecological spaces on the site. The very long benches, the level area suitable for sports, and the generously dimensioned grassland area promise more intense uses in future. The simplicity of the methods and materials employed, such as the reuse of the existing drainage system, reuse of rubble for the multiple purpose room, and the care accorded to the definition of the limited materials is put to work very well, making for a truly robust and economical park. The reinvented agricultural space is part of the project for the urban forest around Mestre. It contributes to renewal of the work on transformation of agricultural land by numerous stakeholders in Veneto and the plain of the Po.

By CZstudio associati Paolo Ceccon Laura Zampieri architects Programme Park Commissioned by Venice municipality Area 8 ha Design 2004–2006 Implementation 2008–2010 Budget € 2,000,000

Structure of the agricultural land reused in the project.

e slope accentuates the existing border of trees.

e path negotiates the limit between the existing wet meadows and
e park.

The lighting, using simple, sturdy elements, gives the park a specific
identity and picks out the main paths by day and by night.

View of the pavilion, looking along the existing ditch.

South edge of the park along the highway.

Sport facilities aligned with the pavilion.

The folding wall becomes a bench.

The pavilion is simultaneously a passage, a shelter and a surface of the park.

Essay by Anna Zahonero

ALTERNATIVE GOLF LANDSCAPES

One of the emerging expressions of urbanites' leisure practices on former agricultural and natural land is the great expansion in the number of golf courses. These are mostly associated with unreasonable consumption of natural resources, or excessive use of herbicides and fertilizers, and jeopardizing more socially accepted uses such as agriculture. However, golf courses can help in the construction of new landscapes, recovery of degraded lands, and efficient control of potentially negative environmental impacts.

A look at the history of golf courses shows us how their design has evolved: starting with the use of natural landscape (in the 1875 Carnoustie Golf Links in Scotland), through the invented landscape of Augusta National (inaugurated in 1934, South Carolina, USA), to the rustic golf course emphasizing its connection with nature, exemplified by the Old Marsh Golf Club (1984, Florida, USA). In each case, the relationship with the landscape where the golf course has been inserted is different, producing more or less complex relations, depending on the specificity of the locality. It is evident that the more powerful the connection with the existing landscape structure, the more successful the integration achieved in terms of energy consumption.

We cannot deny that the extensive use of space by golf courses generates important transformations: places inevitably become 'new places'. But it is at this point that landscape designers are presented with the first challenge: to build a new landscape that may violate the pre-existing dynamics of the place to such an extent that it is virtually impossible to 'mask' – a standard 18-hole golf course requires a minimum of 50 hectares. Coming down to the particular task of golf course landscape design and looking beyond the controversy surrounding golf courses, we need to search for alternatives that are related to the landscape design of a golf course.

GOLF COURSES CAN ENHANCE LANDSCAPE QUALITIES. Golf courses have the potential to reinforce patterns and structures of (valuable and historic) landscapes if these are integrated into the design. The Slovenian office Bruto Landscape Architecture & Design drew up a proposal, called *Back to Nature*, showing how the design of a golf-course can enter into a dialogue with the characteristics of the location. According to the designers this would make the courses less artificial, more natural, and more embedded in the local landscape. The typical natural or cultural landscape would be thus an integral part of the course itself, as it would help to shape fairways, greens, direction of play, and of course hazards. The *Back to Nature* proposal illustrates its approach with three prototypic

ALTERNATIVE GOLF LANDSCAPES

Singelgolf by H+N+S: Much of the territory remains under agricultural use.

Design proposals by Bruto showing how the design of a golf-course can enter into a dialogue with the characteristics of the location.

Real Club de Golf in El Prat, designed by Greg Norman.

case studies: the sustainable, the characteristic and the cultivated landscape. The sustainable golf course takes into account the diversity of habitats and landscapes, and its execution involves little manipulation of space. Whilst the topography remains almost unchanged, the routing is adapted to the characteristics of the area and local habitat. The fairways become narrow and composed of smaller segments, native meadows stretch up to patches of fairway, greens are small and embedded in the existing topography of the terrain. Maintenance of the field is limited to regular mowing of greens and tees, and occasional mowing of the fairway. Fertilizers and plant protection products are not used; watering of the golf course is done with rainwater and is limited to the greens. The designers use the example of a valley with a stream and dead branches of the former riverbed to illustrate the case of a characteristic landscape. The meandering course of the wild river and its dead branches form unique surroundings for the location of a golf course. The routing of the golf course is adapted to the meanders of the stream and vegetation indents of the dead branches so that play takes place in the space between the two main elements of the landscape pattern. As far as the cultivated landscape is concerned, the designers propose a golf course that is adjusted to the orthogonal forms and to the patchwork pattern typical of the agricultural landscapes. The siting of the playing area takes into account land subdivisions and uses. As a result, fairways are shaped for long pitches, and there are many 'dogleg' twisted holes.

The integration of a new use into an existing landscape can be enriched by recognizing valuable extant forms and structural elements of the landscape. However, a new use, such as a golf course, should also take into account the temporal dynamics of an area, and the design should be adapted so that it offers new aesthetics and/or cultural concepts emerging from contemporary social perceptions. Looked at in this way, the design should not only be based on existing morphologies and structures, but also on innovative forms. Another proposal by the Bruto office, called *Forward to the Future*, is an example of golf-course design based on a conceptual imaginary space instead of the characteristics of local landscape. As the designers explain: 'The course therefore is not an artificial Arcadia, trying to be nature itself as happens with most modern courses.'

GOLF COURSES CAN REUSE WASTELANDS. Apart from the potential contribution of the golf course to the conservation of existing valuable ecological/cultural landscapes, one of the most interesting issues is the role of golf-course design in the recovery of degraded lands, especially those located in the periphery of metropolitan areas. These are often areas where infrastructural developments are causing considerable pressure on open space, and where ecological activity and landscape regeneration need to be supported by a designed space and an economic activity that can help finance its maintenance. The golf courses at the Real

Club de Golf in El Prat, outside Barcelona, were designed in 2004 by Greg Norman and address these issues. The aim was to recover the structural elements that had created the image of the location in the past. Once a rich mosaic of agricultural and forest land, it had become degraded and partly abandoned. The design was also intended to stimulate the intrinsic ecological potential of the area. Based on interwoven forest and agricultural units, the design defines the optimum perimeter of contact between these two predominant habitats so that ecological relationships between the forestry and agriculture systems can be restored. The introduction of depressions, where water collects temporarily, has helped improve biodiversity. Although managing and maintaining this reconstructed landscape is not as profitable as agriculture or forestry were in terms of economic returns, the gains are enormous in terms of ecology and landscape recovery, and preservation of the landscape through the introduction of a new use.

GOLF COURSES CAN BE COMBINED WITH OTHER LAND USES.
Golf courses do not necessarily have to replace existing land uses, especially when the existing activities are economically viable. It is possible to organize a golf course to fit into a productive agricultural landscape mosaic or a system of forest exploitation. The concept *Singelgolf*, designed by the Dutch office H+N+S, is an example of this. The idea behind Singelgolf is to use golf as a new driver for regional development. The area in which the golf course would be located is about three times larger than a conventional golf course, but much of the territory remains under agricultural use. The golf course is therefore not an isolated enclave in the landscape, but a new part of it. The core of this new concept is the cooperation between parties that until now have operated independently. Farmers supply the landscape, maintenance and accommodations; the golf business provides the concept and the organization; and of course the golf club contributes with its members. This cooperation can be extended to include other participants, such as hoteliers, riding school owners or environmental associations. The potential benefits of collaboration between various actors in a particular area are interesting. Members of the public may need to be persuaded that they stand to gain from the benefits arising from compatible functions. Golf promoters need to be convinced that landscape and environmental benefits can help create a more interesting golf landscape, in particular for the potential users.

Designers should present the potential of golf courses as generators or regenerators. If we agree that our discipline is multifunctional in essence, and accept the needs of golf as the potential programme to be applied in the landscape, this particular assignment shouldn't be any more complicated than others.

Anna Zahonero Xifré is a professor at the Urbanism and Regional Planning Department of the School of Architecture of Barcelona, where she performs research in the Centre of Landscape Investigation and Design. In 2006 Zahonero started her own company specializing in urban and regional planning, landscape design with

CO-CREATION

SELJORD

MAGDEBURG

LONDON

LISBON

Photo Dag Jenssen

The installations were designed and built at selected sites around the Seljord lake in the autumn of 2009 by students from NABA, Politecnico di Milano and Fredrikstad School of Scenography, during a ten day workshop under the guidance of the architects Sami Rintala and Dagur Eggertsso
Photo Arianna Forcella

SELJORD LAKE SITES

designed by Rintala Eggertsson Architects, Feste Landscape Architects, Springer Kulturstudio

0   2 km

JURY COMMENT This project has everything: respect, good design, poetry, meaning. By paying careful attention to situation, their rustic but still refined design, their gestures that invite immersion in the landscape, these small design projects pay tribute to the fact that landscape architecture is more than shaping physical sites alone – it reaches out into the realm of narratives that exist in people's minds and that condition their landscape experience. In this way, the legends that have been told around the lake for centuries are as much part of the project as the story of the project's evolution in recent years, initiated by European students' drawing and construction, and culminating in the recently inaugurated architecture of a viewing tower. The Seljord landscape occupies such a central position that this project seems to lack a designer's authorship in a common sense – and therefore can be understood as the multi-vocal authorship of people and their narratives.

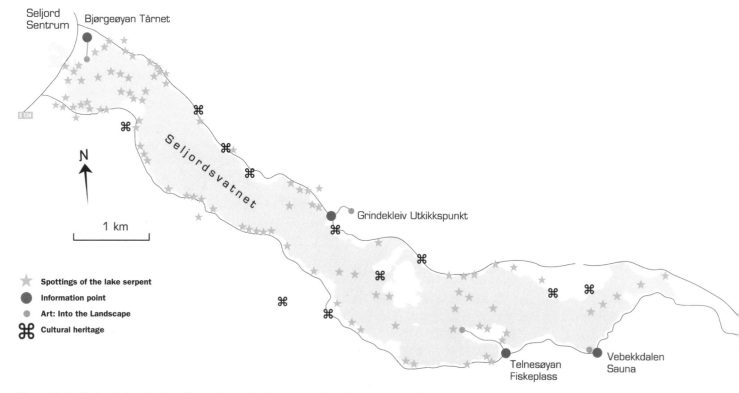

Map of Lake Seljord showing locations where the lake serpent has been observed.

Key:
★ Spottings of the lake serpent
● Information point
● Art: Into the Landscape
⌘ Cultural heritage

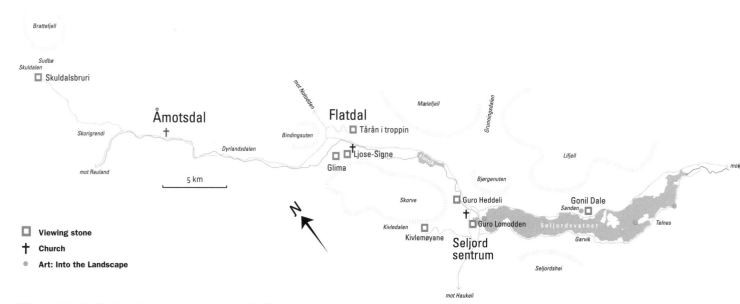

Map of Lake Seljord and the nearby area, showing the locations of viewing stones that recall local legends.

Key:
◻ Viewing stone
✝ Church
● Art: Into the Landscape

Narratives out of and into the landscape

Feature by Alice Labadini

There is a cleft in the rock, somewhere along the shore of Lake Seljord. There, a thin wooden platform has been laid perpendicular to the cut, set down as if penetrating the rock at both ends, bridging the two sides of the cleft. Coming closer, the small bridge also appears to be a roof, defining an open shelter, the base of which is a projection of the same material installed a few metres below, in the cleft. From there, another wooden bridge is situated, connecting the lower platform to the rock and thereby offering access to the sheltered enclosure that is angled towards the lake and ends with a small square barbecue platform, cast in concrete on the bare rock. With its simple but rigorous geometry and its discreet but clear materiality of black painted wooden planks, the installation reveals its presence as an artefact, while it seems to be growing out of the topography, and completing it. The next piece appears at the roadside some kilometres away, initially as a black painted wall installed in a small clearing between the road and the lake. The solidity of its

surface is broken in the middle by a sharply cut opening. By concealing the lake's horizon while cutting out a small glimpse of its foreground, the wall acts, formally, both as a frame and as a threshold. Only upon crossing its boundary, is the view of the lake revealed in its totality, and in doing so one discovers, within the wall itself, the small volume of a wood-fired sauna with a stove.

These installations were designed and built at selected sites around the Seljord lake in the autumn of 2009, by students from from NABA, Politecnico di Milano (Italy) and Fredrikstad School of Scenography (Norway), during a ten-day workshop under the guidance of the architects Sami Rintala and Dagur Eggertsson. Commissioned by the team of designers – Feste Landscape Architects and Springer Kulturstudio – as a part of their project *Seljord and the legends*, these small structures are intended to attract people to visit the landscape around the Seljord lake, and there, perhaps, encounter and engage with its myths.

signing and building the installations involved a close
ation between the site and the drawing board. Photos
anna Forcella

Construction of the fishing point.

In Seljord, tales of a serpent-like creature inhabiting the lake and observations of mysterious phenomena occurring across its surface have been recounted for more than two centuries. The last two installations, a viewing point and a panoramic tower – the latter designed by RintalaEggertsson Architects themselves – are conceived as more explicit references to the visual character of these 'eye-witness' accounts. While the viewing point has been built in an already elevated position, the tower embeds, instead, the physical and symbolic experience of climbing into its very architecture. Each level of the tower is marked with an opening, composing the approach to the top into a sequence of sights over the surroundings. Thus, the view over the lake is made part of a layered time progression, allowing the imagination to travel onwards, after the moment of disclosure, into the landscape and into the myth of the lake serpent. Within this gesture lies a vivid narrative intention.

Seljord and upper Telemark have a rich storytelling tradition. Here, folklore tales have been passed down by word of mouth throughout the centuries, often codified in a distinct rhythm of narration and choice of words. When asked by the local authorities to develop a plan for promoting and regenerating the landscape around Seljord, the regionally based offices Feste and Springer chose to embrace this tradition and placed it at the very core of their proposal. 'Seljord and the legends' is thus a long-term strategy for cultural enhancement as well as a program for interventions in space.

The desire to insert a landscape project into a narrative tradition poses, however, a crucial challenge: that of translating the temporal language and immaterial consistency of storytelling onto the landscape's physical grounds. Instead of a single concept, the project tackles this challenge by layering different strategies, each with individual operative lines and timeframes, linked by a common cartography. The project started by systematically mapping the sites that were related to local tales around the lake and connected to the mountains around Seljord. Granite sculptures make manifest, at each of these sites, the presence of a story. Carved in the shape of human-sized frames, the sculptures are intended to delimit a setting for the tale within the expanse of the surrounding landscape. Simultaneously, it is possible to phone a number and listen to a recorded reading of the same tale.

In the juxtaposition of listening points and installations in the landscape, the project thus constitutes a topology of eventful sequences rather than a consistent spatial plan. According to Feste, the actual linking of the practice of making landscapes to practices of storytelling requires the recognition of the intrinsic capacity of landscapes to engender stories, even outside the agency of a scripted narrative, thus fully embracing the role of the reader as an interpreter and carrier of meaning. In this perspective, the project's discontinuous sequences may be read as a sort of in-situ three-dimensional map, which orients the reader into disclosing and participating in landscape's most intangible entities. A map which is primarily addressed to the eye – proposing a series of visual frames and places for contemplation – but also to the body as a whole, engages with a synaesthetic experience of the territory's indissoluble spatial and memorial fabric.

Reconsidering its individual elements, one can also observe how the project proposes, through its different spatial interventions, compellingly divergent modes of approaching immateriality. On the one hand, the listening posts impart consistency to the intangible matter of narratives by allowing the different stories to 'take place'. The act of locating the story in space, and locating the reader in relation to it, poetically grounds the narration in a physical site. At the same time, the combined agency of the 'viewing stones' and the recorded pieces constructs an environment in which the visitor can be immersed in order to participate in the narration on site. On the other hand, the installations are true openings into the immaterial. Clearly anchored to the site's ground, their presence in nature renders them little more than an added attribute to the topography. With a minimal gesture they encapsulate a vivid condition for human inhabitation, thus creating places, physically but also existentially: places for the visitor to enter, where they are free to pause, to take in the landscape, or be held within. The visitor is confronted with the uncanniness of the landscape as it opens up. Showing without telling, the installations encourage a continuous rewriting of the lake serpent legend by agency of the visitor's imagination and added authorship: 'into the landscape'.

Programme Regeneration of cultural landscape **Designers** Rintala Eggertsson Architects, Feste Landscape Architects, Springer Kulturstudio **Commissioned by** Seljord city council **Area** Scattered locations around the Seljord Lake **Design** 2008–2009 **Implementation** 2009–2011 **Budget** € 610,000 (installations and tower, viewing stones, paths and new signage)

shing point, upper platform. A clear tectonic anchoring to the natural features of the site is a common intention in the design of the installations.
oto Dag Jenssen

Near two ancient pine trees, the volume of the tower negotiates its presence in the landscape. Photos Dag Jenssen

View of the fishing point from the lake.

The sauna is raised above the ground in order to avoid flooding. Piles of stones found on site were used as the base for the sauna's fireplace.

The viewing stones are positioned at distance from the real setting of the story, which is framed inside the stone's looking hole.

thin horizontal cut opens a view from the sauna bench to the lake horizon.

The installation at Grindekleiv Viewpoint is positioned so that it is recessed from the actual outlook, leaving the bedrock untouched as it protrudes over the lake.

A common material language creates a level of visual recognition between the installations. Photo Dag Jenssen

Essay by Lisa Diedrich

One could say that the discipline of landscape architecture has greatly benefitted from the economic and societal developments of 20th-century Europe. This is manifest in a body of outstanding projects built over the last three decades all over the continent. Internationally acclaimed and widely published examples were selected for and reflected upon in the three editions of the Landscape Architecture Europe book series. However, experiencing the current economic and social turbulence one might also suspect that this glorious epoch is coming to an end and ask how long we should continue to regard landscape architectural work as an answer to this 'post-industrial' era and evolving from 'post-modern' thought. In Europe, post-modernism is primarily understood as arising in opposition to modernism, being associated with the closing down of heavy industry and the denial of universal design and tabula rasa attitudes. Indeed, the former era has named the latter and therefore still qualifies it. Inherited words testify to inherited discourses – so even in 2012 we haven't completely left the 20th century. But new words are emerging, novel arguments are entering the debate, and some promising yet unfamiliar landscape architectural works can be observed, of which *Seljord Lake Sites*, the *Open Air library*, *Normand Park* and *Tagus cycle track* are examples. They might finally indicate to us wondrous ways into the 21st century.

Maybe we should call them 'wandering ways' and accompany French art critique Nicolas Bourriaud on some of them. In his 2009 essay *The Radicant* he refers to Jacques Lacan's idea of the *erre*, the wandering, easily associated with 'erratic', even 'erroneous' movement, but which is understood as positive, as a driving force on the threshold to promise: '(The *erre*) is something like momentum. The momentum something has when what was formerly propelling it stops.' (Bourriaud 2009, p. 93) So we could say that the modern engine has stopped, the car keeps going, and we are caught in the forward motion initiated by modernism, sitting in the car and trying to find a different fuel, trying to run it according to the present topography, along wondrous ways, wandering... In which direction might become clearer, the more the forward motion slows down. For when something stops, something else emerges. In order to see and shape what emerges, we might have to cease looking back and naming our epoch post-modern, out of the wish to rid ourselves of the forward-looking modern ideology. Only then will we be able to acknowledge and become involved with where we live now, in this present moment: in a globalized world. Globalization is the phenomenon that, since the collapse of the communist bloc in 1989, has embraced all of the world's societies. Going beyond familiar studies of globalization from social, economic and political points of view, Nicolas Bourriaud takes a fresh look at the *aesthetics* of globalization, surveying contemporary works of art and how globalization impacts the 'life of *form*'. His new vocabulary, elaborated from close analyses of works of art, also proves extremely helpful for identifying and qualifying works of landscape architecture that deviate from the trajectory of the run-down engine and engage with new driving forces.

'Altermodernity' is the word Bourriaud suggests as a name for the field we are currently exploring. In doing so, he accepts the fact that we have not yet left 20th-century thinking (the run-down engine), but at the same time situates us within an alternative state of mind (the new driving forces), even though he does not name the content of this alternative. When browsing the claims of architects and landscape architects of the postmodern period, it is easy to identify them as answers to modernism and one feels the urge to finally close this chapter and start asking for alternatives: alternative ethics, alternative aesthetics, and also alternative self-conceptions for landscape architects and other designers. One activity we would do better to bring to an end is the search for origins, for roots, for the essence of things as a motor of design. Christian Norberg Schulz' book *Genius Loci* written in 1979 is the best known theoretical statement of this tendency, detecting archetypes (the cosmic, the classical, the romantic landscape) in precise geographical regions (the north African desert, southern Europe, the north of Europe) as the essence from which building should derive its inspiration. Art theoretician Mari Hvattum observes the same 'tyranny of site' (Hvattum 2010) in recent works by architects and landscape architects where for example only stones from local quarries are used, or endemic plants. The other conviction that needs to be overcome is the belief in facts, figures and quantified items as the motor of design. This tendency can be observed in Ian McHarg's seminal book *Design with Nature* (1969), which starts from the wish to make nature scientific and therefore acceptable to planners, then dissecting it into various layers such as geology, surface hydrology, botany and climate, and suggesting that landscape architects process these facts into building directives. In recent times, 'data school' architects like MVRDV claim to derive their designs directly and exclusively from data, claiming that a building or a landscape be a spatialized collection of facts and figures. In the first case, the essentialist position, the designer is considered a medium with metaphysical capacities – obscuring his or her reasoning. In the second case, the positivistic position, the designer is seen as an accountant running an operation system – negating his or her sensitive skills. Both positions are deterministic, because the designer is defined as somebody who has no choice other than to build from origins or from facts.

rences
Nicolas Bourriaud, The
cant, 2009 (Original French
on: Nicolas Bourriaud, *Radi-*
Pour une esthétique de la
alisation, 2009).

hristian Norberg Schulz,
us Loci. Towards a Phenom-
ogy of Architecture, 1979.

Mari Hvattum, 'Stedets
ni', in *Arkitekten 2*, pp. 33-
2010.

an McHarg, *Design with*
re, 1969.

MVRDV, *Metacity/Datatown*,
9.

While these positions may elucidate the radical post-modern answers to the radical modern ethics and aesthetics, they do not help us much further today. In a globalized world with its ceaseless flows of goods, information and persons, the question of origin is mostly irrelevant, and the computing of facts and figures is taken for granted. It is here that Bourriaud invites us to challenge the proper radicality of modernism and post-modernism – the obsession of beginning from scratch or from history, the growing of new roots or sticking to old ones – and introduces a pragmatic alternative, based on the following metaphor:

'To remain within the vocabulary of the vegetable realm, one might say that the individual of these early years of the 21st century resembles those plants that do not depend on a single root for their growth but advance in all directions on whatever surfaces present themselves by attaching multiple hooks to them, as ivy does. Ivy belongs to the botanical family of the *radicants*, which develop their roots as they advance, unlike the *radicals*, whose development is determined by their being anchored in a particular soil.' (Bourriaud 2009: 51)

Immigrants, exiles, tourists, commuters, urban wanderers seem to Bourriaud to be the dominant figures of the globalized world, and *radicant* is the name he gives to their way of anchoring and translating themselves into the spaces they enter. They have their roots somewhere – these are the first ones – and then they need to settle elsewhere, so they grow secondary roots, which adapt to the particular soil they find in the places they happen to arrive. Radicants are in a constant dialogue and in constant motion. They are 'caught between the need for a connection with (their) environment and the forces of uprooting, between globalization and singularity, between identity and the opening to the other.' (Bourriaud: ibid) Within this field of shifting sand, nothing is determined; everything is negotiable.

Negotiating is exactly the task of landscape architects and other designers today. If we want to overcome deterministic figures of thought and subscribe to a pragmatic approach focusing on attitudes towards the present moment, we might well develop radicant design as a relational, dialogic and dynamic form of intervention on sites we negotiate to work with. Many of the sites landscape architects deal with today are fall-outs of the industrial epoch: post-industrial wastelands, dysfunctional districts or forgotten worlds, such as the remote Lake Seljord area in southern Norway, the shrinking urban district in East Germany's Magdeburg, the multi-ethnic low-income neighbourhood around Normand Park in West London, the strip of half-abandoned harbour areas along the River Tagus in Lisbon. None of these sites allowed for radical 20th century design because they were overwhelmingly far away, poor, socially complicated or in a pending state of transformation. Characterized by precarious conditions, they were simply not classical sites for classical projects.

Radicant design can make do with these sites. Instead of creating an oeuvre, radicant design evolves along with continuous inquiries, interventions and evaluations into a dialogue. This evolution and the related design processes are as much part of the work as the various elements, persons, materials, events, memories and atmospheres. The work cannot be described as a classical form; it is a progressing form. Its authorship is blurred: the classical framework of designers, clients and public no longer fits – all are co-creators. Not that these evolutive and cooperative work modes would be unfamiliar to landscape architects – on the contrary, but they didn't propel 20th century landscape discourses. Let's do so now with Bourriaud, who calls the ethical mode of altermodernity 'translation' and its aesthetical expression the 'journey-form'. Performative aspects are easily part of a journey-form, as the *Seljord Lake Sites* project shows – a forgotten place where both the legends of old and the international students' building activities form the landscape architectural work, to say nothing of the experience of being on the (wondrous) ways that link these minimalistic interventions. The work takes place rather than form. Social aspects of the post-colonial neighbourhood are the driving force of *Normand Park's* design, again a journey-form in its process of evolution to open civic space, along which the landscape architects brought into dialogue such different neighbours as the old Brits who had experienced the site's bombing, which was the origin of the open space, the various school children's gardening ideas, and the black teenagers' longing for stage setting. All are co-designers of the work. The same is the case in the *Open-air library* project, an urban fall-out of the former GDR, where the willpower of the remaining inhabitants together with the inventive talent of the young designers generate a still consolidating open-air library from a once improvised book and beer crate stack. The growing solidarity is as much part of the journey-form as the interest in reading and the evolving materials of the open urban space. Finally, the designers of the *Tagus Cycle Track* through the extended harbour wastelands on Lisbon's riverfront built a bike trail across the formerly fenced-off areas from almost nothing. Asphalt, kerbstones, painted orientation signs and literature quotes enter into dialogue with material, memories and ambiances found on site and attract cyclists and strollers who in turn continue to appropriate the site in various ways rather than awaiting the official transformation. The current unpredictability of urban development is a great advantage of this journey-form. The work is underway. We do not yet know where the *erre*, the wandering, will take us, but meanwhile radicant landscape architecture helps us to root in unfamiliar grounds.

Lisa Diedrich is editor-in-chief of the *Landscape Architecture Europe* series and professor of landscape architecture at

TAGUS CYCLE TRACK

designed by Global Arquitectura Paisagista and P06

A cycle path where city and river meet. Photos João Delgado da Silveira Ramos

Initiated by the municipality of Lisbon, this project presents a cycle path where city and River Tagus meet. The trail is based on the use of multiple signs, surfaces and spatial configurations all of which represent events bearing witness to a riparian space with a memory, to be reinvested today as the route is experienced, also in the minds of the users. Letters and pictograms printed on and alongside the track guide cyclists on their journeys through the site and its (hi)stories. The landscape architect's attentive reading revolves around expressing the traces and textures of the existing terrain and facades of buildings by selecting and introducing materials and markings, all of which are signs open to the users' interpretation. Unfurling layer by layer, this intervention makes skilful use of the cycle track route to create a strong experience that appeals to the collective imagination of the people of Lisbon. [tk]

Programme Bike trail **Designer** Global Arquitectura Paisagista (João Gomes da Silva) and P06 (Nuno Gusmão, designer) **Commissioned by** Lisbon Port Administration APL, Municipality of Lisbon and EDP **Area** 63,000 m² **Design** 2008–2009 **Implementation** 2009 **Budget** € 1,000,000

Words on the cycle path illustrate the sounds of the 25 April bridge.

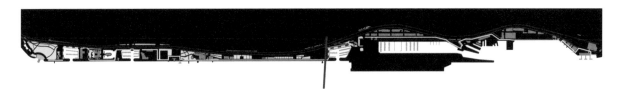

The track along the water.

designed by Kinnear Landscape Architects

NORMAND PARK

Animated tree lighting sequence, created by involved teenagers. Photos Mark Thomas

Situated in the west of London in a district with a diverse range of incomes and ethnic backgrounds, this park redesign project seeks to use community engagement as the main driver, giving local people a new focus for their community through provision of a community café and community-run gardens as well as cross-generation and natural play opportunities. The designers are part of a creative, collaborative undertaking that aimed to mobilize all possible potentials from site in an extraordinarily imaginative way. Design concepts, spaces and park elements were conceived in four projects: one with primary school children to explore modes of play and the history of cultivation; one with older residents who remembered the houses they lived in on this site and how the park came into being from a bomb site; and one through a photography and film project with teenagers who explored their identity as people in the park. The latter project developed further, and the teenagers became involved in creating an interactive lighting installation. The landscape architects structured the park with two intersecting routes linking key district buildings: the Broadwalk, featuring etched extracts of the memory project, and the Play Path, complete with an open lawn with mounds for flexible use, community gardens, and equipped play areas. [ld]

The Broadwalk, crossing north to south.

Programme Redesign of a neighbourhood park **Designer** Kinnear Landscape Architects **Arts workshops by** Gayle Chong Kwan (artist), Paul Shepheard (writer), Faisal Abdu Allah (artist), Jason Bruges Studio (lighting) **Commissioned by** London Borough of Hammersmith and Fulham/North Fulham New Deal for Communities, Arts Council England and Big Lottery (lighting art installation) **Area** 2 ha **Design** 2006–2007 **Implementation** 2007–2008 **Budget** € 2,041,410 (plus € 40,828 for lighting arts installation)

OPEN AIR LIBRARY

designed by KARO*

A 'social sculpture' in a city in heavy economic decline. Photo Anja Schlamann

This project, dubbed 'social sculpture' by its authors, is derived from the idea of creating a communal library as a participative, self-managed action by the inhabitants of a city in heavy economic decline where building unoccupancy rates are as high as 80 percent. Initially, a temporary open air library had been installed in a public square using a thousand ingeniously stacked beer crates and donated books. When the inhabitants made the project permanent by opening an informal library in a building near the initial site, the KARO* designers were asked to think up an adjacent public space incorporating a stage, using salvaged material. The mixture of a co-conception scheme – unconventional in today's Europe – and the reuse of highly conventional materials, salvaged from the demolition of a large prefabricated 1960s facade and simply repainted, convinced the jury. [tk]

Programme Public square with an informal outdoor library and open air stage **Designer** KARO* (Antje Heuer, Stefan Rettich, Bert Hafermalz) **In collaboration with** Architektur+Netzwerk (Sabine Eling-Saalmann) **Commissioned by** City of Magdeburg **Area** 488 m² **Design** 2008–2009 **Implementation** 2009 **Budget** € 325,000

Stacked beer crates form the open air library.

A shared public space.

RURAL PLACES

SERMANGE^{WEIACH}

The new wooden bench in front of the church.

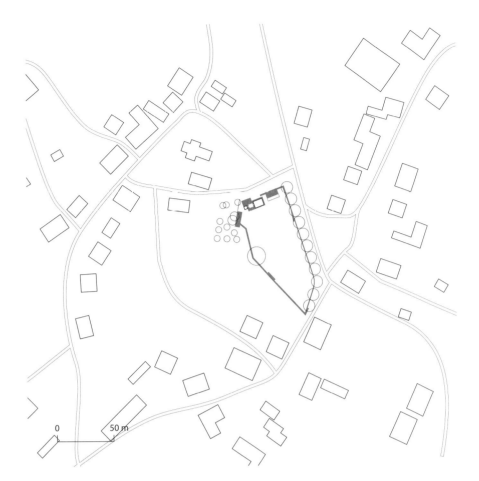

0   50 m

JURY COMMENT Whereas all too often village greens have been transformed into 'city-like' centres, in Sermange a low-key intervention was opted for. The designers went for the only right solution. The design confines itself to demarcating the open space, which has been there for centuries and is held dear by the village and its inhabitants. The effect is sophisticated, and nowhere is this clearer than in the precise way in which the course of the boardwalk follows the topography of the landscape.

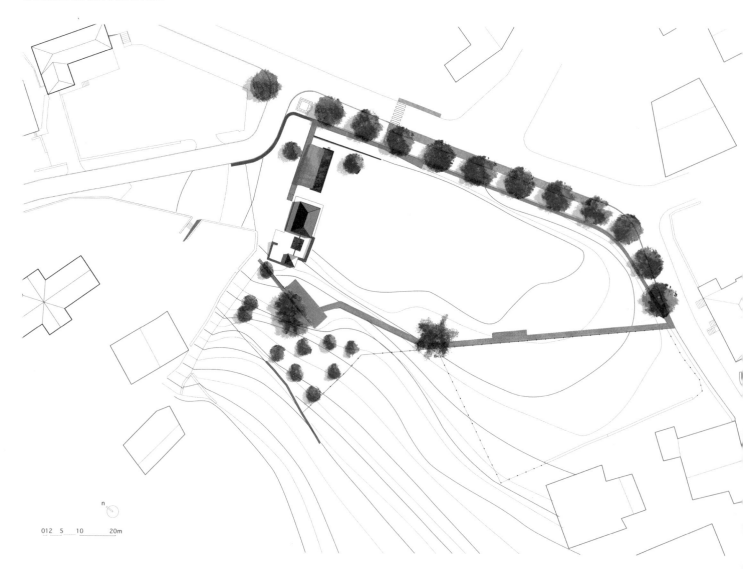

012 5 10 20m

Design.

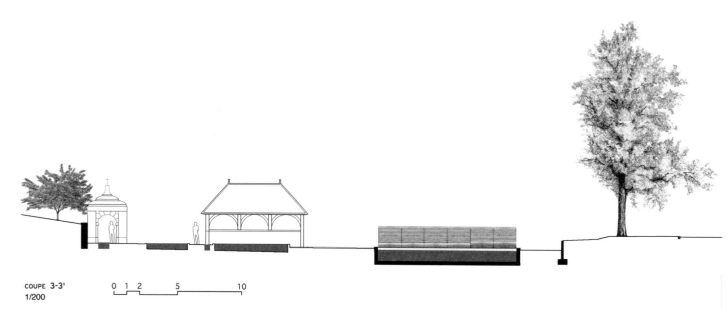

COUPE **3-3'**
1/200

0 1 2 5 10

Cross-section at the level of the old washhouse.

Designing a village's central void

Feature by Mark Hendriks

The village green occupies the most prominent location in the rural community of Sermange in the French Jura. An empty grass field in the shadow of the church, the terrain forms a natural depression where rainwater collects from the surrounding hills. Because of the high groundwater level the green has never been built on. Yet this apparently meaningless 'bit of land' actually has great significance for the small community of Sermange, which numbers about 240 souls. On its northern edge lie two natural springs, which in times gone by were a source of drinking water and also supplied water to the washhouse and fountain, both of which are still present. The green is the stage for big events. From Bastille day on the 14th of

July and other traditional celebrations to fireworks shows at New Year and the efforts of the national football team: people gravitate towards the field near the church for all of these events. The bare meadow has also gained significance further afield, having been a node in a regional cycle network for some years now.

A few years ago the Sermange village council decided to redesign the heart of their village. In the councillors' view, its dullness did not do justice to the significant role it plays in village community life. The councillors felt that a location of such value to the village deserved to be upgraded in terms of orientation and landscaping so that it

aerial view shows clearly how only the edges have been demarcated, accentuating the open space in the middle.

would become a more integral part of the village. A design was commissioned from the landscape architects at Agence Territoires in Besançon and it was implemented in 2008.

The first impression is that little has changed since then, for the centre of Sermange is still dominated by the empty expanse in front of the beautiful white church, with, in the northern corner, the spring and next to it *la grande fontaine* and the limestone washhouse. This embodies the essence of Agence Territoires' design concept for this 'heart of the village'. The emptiness and subdued landscaping are not the unwished-for consequence of a lack of functions and elements. Rather, the field's emptiness is its strength, as it introduces clarity and structure into the organic structure of the village. In this void lie the rural origins of the settlement – like the common in the historical heart of the megacity of Boston or the quintessential English village green.
The field is bounded on the east by a regional road, a plateau in the north-west corner (upon which the church stands) and a property line on the western side. The design interventions are concentrated along these edges, which have been emphasized to accentuate the feeling of open space in the middle. The new edge reaffirms the presence of the low-lying grass field that forms the heart of Sermange: the sharply delineated yet transparent border makes it clear where the area starts and ends – without losing its relationship with the surrounding village.

Halfway up the slope in the north-western corner – on the spot where until recently a farm stood – a picnic area has been made, with a view over the green and the village. The concrete picnic table has the same dimensions as the tables in the village community centre and, when the weather permits, the tables can be placed end to end for festivities or meetings. From the picnic area a wooden boardwalk runs along the western edge to the southernmost point. Formally the boardwalk forms a dividing line between the field and the adjacent private land. But the flowing walkway emphasizes much more the relief of the area, tracing where the sloping land flattens out into the low-lying area. The boardwalk is supported by wooden stakes of equal length, maintaining the same distance between the walkway and the ground. Thus walkers experience, consciously or unconsciously, the undulations in the landscape. In the previous situation a side road of the relatively busy regional road cut through the north-eastern corner of the green. This has been rerouted, as a result of which the northern side now has a more logical border: a footpath of brushed concrete separates the road and the green from each other. Ash trees have been planted along the path, but their high crowns mean that the view between the green and the houses on the other side of the road is not obstructed.

The northern edge of the green is bounded by the springhouse, the fountain and the washhouse. To these existing structures a rectangular pond has been added, for two reasons. First, the new water feature is a reference to the groundwater, which flows via this corner in the direction of a nearby stream. Second, the pond forms a contemporary capstone to the series of historical reflections of water use. The spring itself was a source of drinking water for the villagers, the fountain was where livestock drank and the washhouse water was used for household tasks. The new pond is a manifestation of the contemporary role of water: relaxation and recreation. The design is modern – a concrete pond with decking and a wooden bench. Each component is therefore distinct, in terms of material, form, colour and function. The wide open space in the middle of the green has a compensatory effect on the mix of architectonic expressions along the edges. The overview it provides helps visitors to orient themselves, wherever their vantage point.

If the village council had got its way, a whole 'programme' would have been added to the grass field, including a terrace, hard surfaces, a fountain and a playground too. The idea of retaining the grass field met with resistance: councillors *and* residents felt that there was already enough grass in the village. But the then mayor was in favour of Agence Territoires' proposal. He understood that the daring option of leaving the open field as it was and emphasizing its edges was the only way – given the rural character of Sermange – to define the central space. As a result of the mayor's persistence and the sensitive eye of the designers, the temptation was resisted to sacrifice a magnificent open space in the middle of a country village for just another village square. Nevertheless, three pieces of playground equipment were added last year, just in front of the old washhouse. On the insistence of the designers these were moved to the orchard on the slope above the picnic area.

Programme Refurbishment of a central green, fountain and washhouse **Designer** Agence Territoires **Commissioned by** Village of Sermange **Area** 0.64 ha **Design** 2007 **Implementation** 2008 **Budget** € 235,000

modern design of the pond, decking and bench invites relaxation recreation.

Football is a favourite pastime on the green.

Sermange village green. On the right: the regional road.

Halfway down the slope is a picnic area.

The boardwalk traces the transition in topography, where the sloping land flattens out.

The pond extends the line that ended with the historic washhouse.

e wooden decking near the old wash house.

Walkers experience the undulations of the landscape.

THE POWER OF DISCRETE CHANGE

Essay by Ana Kučan

In past years, rural landscapes have been subjected to accelerated transformation throughout Europe, resulting in fragmentation and melting identities. As the immediate connection between settlements and agricultural land has been abandoned in many cases, new landscape patterns and housing typologies have emerged. Design interventions intended to improve the spatial character of rural communities often fail to do so, instead they destroy significance, meaning and qualities by being either too bold or out of place. Comfort and form seem to prevail over social and ecological concerns. Without a thorough inquiry into the causes of this failure one can only speculate on the nature of what could be termed a proper intervention. The topic of the appropriate in design is very complex and open-ended. Nevertheless, contemporary environmental and social issues require approaches that are sustainable. Not in the sense of that rather abused ecological term, but in the sense of *sustainability* which denotes holding back, to abstain consciously in situations which require so. Challenges we are facing may change our understanding of design; may it then become possible to view a decision to restrain as a creative action? Anyway, it does seem that in rural ambiences one should defer from actions of total transformation; they, in many cases, seem neither needed nor appropriate. Again, however,…can we ever define what appropriate is?

LANDSCAPE IDENTITY. The definition of landscape is broad and ever growing. Originally, the word *landschaft* signified the territory over which we move and the space of relationships we create while living on the surface of the earth. In its essence, this definition still applies: the concept of landscape is deeply and widely connected to the concept of dwelling and identity. When designing, one always encounters the problem of defining the identity of the landscape one is about to change. Emerging from physical realities, landscape identities are no less social constructs, forming a base for our interaction with the landscape – in order to recognize the character, to understand the patterns we need to be able to read the space, to catch its *spirit*.[1] Let us assume that this *spirit of place* is nothing other than the human conception of it. Thus it implies one's ability to penetrate mentally through the superficial appearance of any spatial formation. Certain knowledge is required for one to do so, the ability to recognize the potential of the existing landscape for its very change into something new.

Landscape architecture is a body of knowledge which concerns the material change of nature into designed landscapes including the transformation into the act of design. Here we must make our first distinction. We are not talking about formation of new landscapes but about the transformation of the existing ones. Each act, each insertion of an artefact transforms the landscape; even naming it transforms it, as *landscape* is a cultural construct and as such exists even before the actual physical transformations of the ground take place. As an illustration let me use the metaphor of the Wallace Stevens' jar which 'made the slovenly wilderness' … 'no longer wild' and although the jar 'was grey and bare' it 'took dominion every where':

I placed a jar in Tennessee
And round it was, upon a hill.
It made the slovenly wilderness
Surround that hill.

The wilderness rose up to it,
and sprawled around, no longer wild.
The jar was round upon the ground
And tall and of a port in air.

It took dominion every where.
The jar was gray and bare.
It did not give of bird or bush,
Like nothing else in Tennessee.
(Wallace Stevens, 1954)

Now we need to make our second distinction. Contrary to architecture, which has the advantage to create *ab ovo*, designed landscapes are always contextual. Although architecture has recently discovered the ground, the fact is that doing so is not intrinsic to it while in landscape design it is inevitable. Even when we change the ground completely and create a totally new entity with no reference to what was there before, the problems solved in the process are originated by their physical characteristics which in turn are subject to natural processes. This is even more so when the object of transformation is a landscape with a distinct and recognizable character.[2]

By (re)designing landscape in rural areas one is dealing with landscapes which already have strong identity. With landscapes, where *utilitas, firmitas, venustas*[3] have already been achieved. Interventions change them. Fine: identity itself is a changeable phenomenon. The question is how we change it, which design language is appropriate to express the meaning of the intervention and what one wants to say in the first place.

VISUAL LANGUAGE. When talking about language, in order to understand the means of expression, one needs to locate landscape intervention as programme translated into physi-

he concept was years
beautifully brought to the
ation by Norberg-Schultz. In
980s, the concept gained
ning nearing the spiritual
failed as a serious method.
rtheless it can be seen as
objective demand to read
space before changing it
the design action, which
es the book a still widely
text book in architectural
ols. Christian Norberg-
ltz, *Genius Loci. Towards
Phenomenology of Architec-
 1979.

he question of landscape
city, which inevitably rises
n the process of planning,
ore or less related to the
al and cultural identities
e population living in and
ing within these precise
scapes. The inherited
tion is consciously or un-
ciously involved in the
ation of their relationship
rds the landscapes and
e way they change or pre-
e them. More in Ana
n, 'Constructing Land-
e Conceptions', in *JoLA,
al of Landscape Architec-
 spring 2007, pp. 38-49.

irmitas in landscape archi-
ure meaning natural proc-
s sustaining landscape,
g either suppressed or (re)
ted by maintenance.

imon Schama, *Landscape
Memory*, 1995.

ee Raymond Quenaeu,
rcises du Style*, 1947.

cal reality in the realm of landscape design possibilities. Only through this can one understand the way of transforming a design action into a visual language. Here we first encounter the concern with the autonomy and number of languages of landscape design, their compositional qualities and their inherent and possible meanings. And, talking about what is appropriate, it is important to understand that what is appropriate to some may not be appropriate to others. Here universality of language is put on hold, stories told tend to be rather local. At issue – and not only in rural areas – are formal possibilities made legible by the use of conventions. The conventions in language are vocabulary and syntax, in our case they are the elements of design and its compositional principles, which offer means of expression. Which means of expression are essentially autonomous to landscape design? Answers can be found in 'Wood, Water, Rock', each of which is a chapter title of Simon Schama's study of the ways of looking into and disclosing, as he himself says, 'the veins of myth and memory that lie beneath the surface'.[4] They are *trees, water, ground*, a vocabulary used by heroic transformations of old landscapes into new ones alluding to rural pastures and to the Arcadian myth in order to communicate the new concept of the society. Those were total transformations; the need for the New Landscape expressing new aspirations caused the (r)evolution of the vocabulary and compositional principles. Landscapes that Lancelot Brown built had an expression essentially autonomous to landscape design's way of constructing space and thus creating a recognizable design language. The elements used still form the base of Western landscape imagery. Yet none of the rural projects published in this book uses this imagery directly. Why is this so? They are dealing with landscapes which already have strong identity, the imagery mentioned is already there. Both, the intervention in Sermange, *Heart of the village* and the one in Weiach (*Stadlerstrasse*) are more about objects inserted in landscape than about landscape change in its true sense. Yet the effect of these design interventions is as strong as the intervention is subtle; they are like a jar, acting by the power of *discrete change*.

The issue I try to address is the issue of *fitting into*, to intervene in the strict sense of the word, while enhancing the existing character of the place with new meaning precisely by the withdrawal from bold design action. This kind of approach can, as demonstrated by selected examples, add to the expressive power of the existing and through that change it. In no way do 'restricted actions', as we may call them, negate looking for new possibilities in development and use of visual language; on the contrary, they are tangible proof of the everlasting insistence on exploring new formal and figurative possibilities and on reinterpreting traditional conventions, which goes well beyond borrowing or applying the same simple measures from a 'catalogue of types'. In the baroque, the vocabulary was limited and the syntax was clear and simple, yet they led to magnificent, cosmic landscapes, unprecedented and unrepeatable. Restrictions in vocabulary or syntax do not imply a limitation in expression.[5]

DIRECTION TO GO. Both projects, in Sermange and in Weiach, are interventions in the landscape in the truest sense of the word. In both cases the materiality of the insertion literally fits into the existing, picking up the local *narrative* and continuing the story. They have not changed the character of what already existed beyond its accepted recognition; they are about subtlety and sensibility, which in cases of interventions in established cultural landscapes should be a guiding principle for the process of landscape change which culminates in the act of design – leading from the ability to read the landscape up to the decision of how to edit it, involving the materialization of the design ideas.

Design actions in established cultural landscapes relate to discourses of local identity and place. One should first of all recognize the vocabulary and the composition principles which are already there. These may be hidden to the eye, thus one needs to explore the complexity of the place beyond formal issues. Only then one can articulate it, or rather re-articulate, transform and permute it while creating a new spatial structure, in order to bring to life the story of the place by telling it anew.

Ana Kucan, PhD, is a landscape architect and principal of AKKA. She is also professor of landscape architecture

STADLERSTRASSE

Technical interventions have been used to open up the space in the centre of Weiach.

A creative solution for an everyday problem: the redesign of a through-road in Weiach was an opportunity to transform the busy street that ran through the centre of the village into a pleasant and well-ordered place to be. The design yields a win-win situation: traffic safety has been increased and the centre of the village has become more attractive. Predominantly technical interventions, such as widening the road, cutting down trees and shrubs, repaving and a new bus stop, have been used to open up the space – strengthening visual relations between the town hall, the school and other public buildings. Longitudinal rectangular concrete elements have been placed in the road. These serve as traffic islands for pedestrians, a signal to approaching cars to slow down, and they frame the new bus stop. The autonomy of the design can be questioned, however. If the new design had had a truly positive influence on the behaviour of the traffic – as was the intention – then the yellow marker posts at the head of the concrete elements would not have been necessary. [mh]

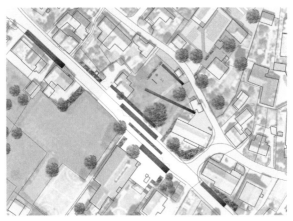

Ground plan.

Programme Redesign of a village's main street and through-road **Designer** vi.vo.architecture.landscape **In collaboration with** Gregor Trachsel (bus stop) **Commissioned by** Municipality of Weiach, Canton Zurich **Area** 0.1 ha **Design** 2005–2009 **Implementation** 2009 **Budget** € 74,000

FRIESLAND

TWENTE

RESEARCH BY DESIGN

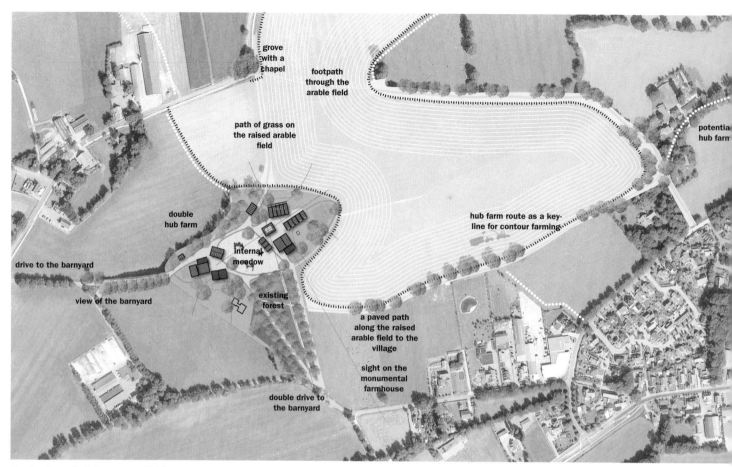

Design for a hub farm near Tubbergen.

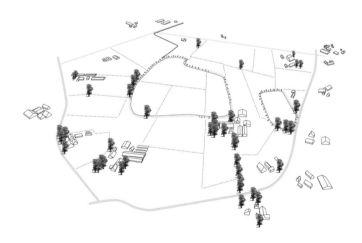

Present situation: fragmented landscape.

Previous pages: Example of a hub farm: Erve Oostermaat designed by Franz Ziegler.
Photo Harry Harsema

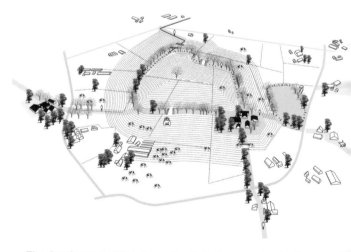

The develoment of Hub farms leads to increased cohesion, creati opportunities for large-scale farming in a small-scale landscape.

HUB FARMS

designed by van Paridon X de Groot

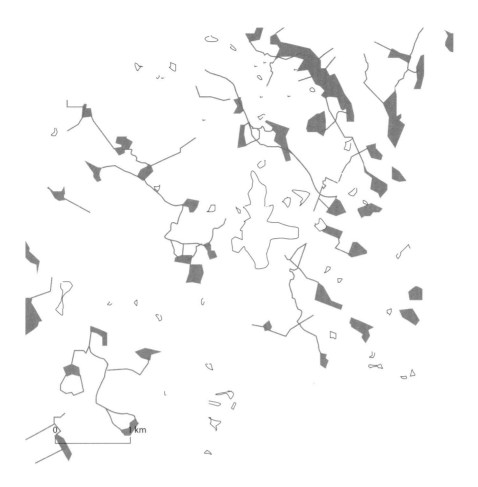

0   1 km

JURY COMMENT Landscape architects are particularly well prepared for tackling spatial development issues in thinking across all scales and for overcoming the still widely accepted assumption of a duality of urban and rural areas. Fighting current sprawl by proposing to re-use farms and increase the accessibility of the agricultural landscape, this approach deals with the development of the cultural landscape as a single space of action. In order to succeed however, this strategy needs critical mass and the construction of a network of hub farms, which will have consequences that would need to be evaluated at large scale. Van Paridon X de Groot present a very sensible and sensitive piece of research on the potential of the agricultural landscape to combine new farming and dwelling modes and to counteract an unplanned growth of the urban periphery. One hopes that this project will trigger many follow-ups in other European regions.

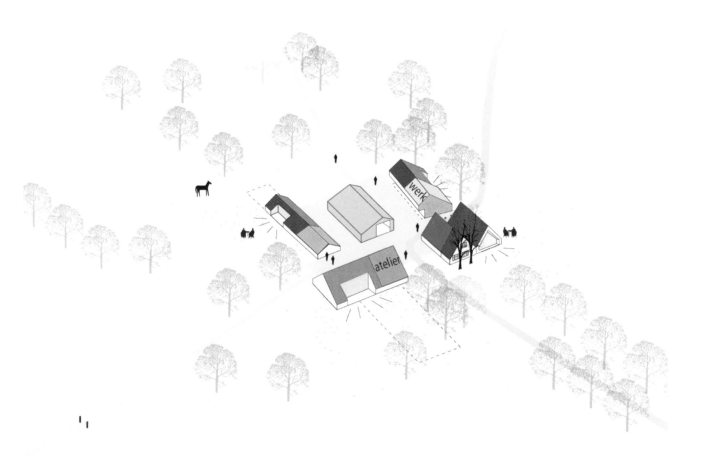

A farmyard is transferred into a collection of mixed buildings.

Farmers' property   Hub farm property   Farmers' property

Shared landscape management.

A cultural landscape for urban dwelling and farming

Feature by Thierry Kandjee

Thousands of farms cease production every year and the space they occupied is being taken over by diffuse urbanization. Remaining farms increase in size, adding to the risk of urban sprawl. Although the phenomenon is well known and an ongoing issue on a European scale, it has prompted little concern on the part of stakeholders so far. In the rural area of Overijssel in the east of the Netherlands, out of 26,000 existing farms, only 10,000 are in the possession of farmers, and two-thirds of these are expected to go out of business at some point in the future. The fate of farmland is under discussion.

The project developed by the landscape architects van Paridon X de Groot presents an innovative vision of the possible future development of the countryside, representing a new way of thinking in particular with regard to a re-invention of how agricultural space is shared and used by people. The main feature of the van Paridon X de Groot approach is the presentation of an overall strategy for the region based on specific case studies, the

question being how to develop agriculture while facilitating the settlement of newcomers who have new ideas and aspirations about life in the countryside. Based on detailed reconnaissance of the land, due consideration of socioeconomic factors, and identification of a network of players with the skills to initiate the project, van Paridon X de Groot proposes a 'hub farm' prototype which informs the project's overall strategy in a consistent manner. This remarkable and wide-reaching process illustrates the capacity of landscape architects to propose innovative and inspiring solutions that engage with society's needs, and it constitutes an example of the potential for renewal and disciplining of landscape architecture.

The region south of Twente, part of Overijssel, is composed of medium-sized farms (20 to 60 hectares) surrounded by forested paths and estates. Part of the legacy of an agriculture marked by successive change, raised fields (called '*essen*') are one of the structural elements of the countryside around which the farms are grouped. Where

 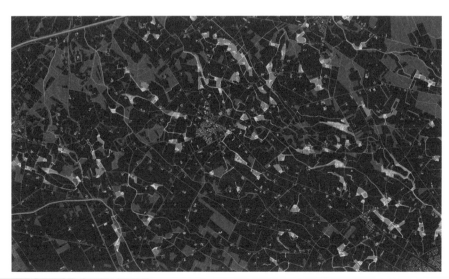

ecific landscape structure. Photo Peter van Bolhuis, Pandion   **Hub farm development strategy.**

the agricultural paths cross, the farmyards form a strong relationship with the landscape. For van Paridon X de Groot, a sensitive reading of this particular morphology, which creates identity while upholding a variety of usages and practices, is the foundation upon which the project is based.

The crux of the strategy is the 'hub-farm': farms where agriculture is no longer the only or main activity are developed to include new housing and workspaces. The new group of inhabitants assumes responsibility for the small-scale elements in the landscape, while the remaining farmers in the surrounding area take care of the management of open space. The farmers are allowed to continue their operations – mainly dairy – while incorporating the dynamics of urban developments. On the one hand, farmers need more space than they can obtain from the hub-farms. On the other hand, city dwellers are looking for an alternative to settlement in the urban periphery, and seeking a different quality of life in the countryside that would not be feasible today in an urban setting. A study by De Groot and Van Paridon based on cartography and presented in their 2003 thesis at the Amsterdam Academy of Architecture (Academie van Bouwkunst Amsterdam) points toward a number of alarming phenomena. Urbanization of the countryside is contingent upon legislation. The progressive disappearance of fine agricultural holdings over the past 50 years due to the expansion of agriculture has led to progressive fragmentation of the countryside. In association with urban sprawl, these are the main issues that have been identified.

The principles underlying the proposal are simple. A farmer who gives up his farm may sell his land to neighbours who need to expand. As plots with buildings tend to be too large for a single person to acquire, the proposal is to retain the typology of the existing farms and renovate or convert them by enabling groups of owners to purchase them, which is not allowed in under existing legislation. In this rural context, conversion of the farms would attract new residents, services and facilities. Apart from simple group purchase, new occupiers would be required to manage the agricultural paths designated for restoration. In that way, the new occupier is at the same time a manager of open space and guarantees the permeability of the road network, the public routes that keep the land viable.

From strategy to action: van Paridon X de Groot's proposal is expressed in game rules, outlining ways to achieve a number of objectives. These include strengthening countryside features through sustained countryside management; developing

agricultural surface areas while maintaining plots; providing a diverse range of accommodation, work, recreational and personal care activities; improving the accessibility of rural areas. In particular, the game rules address the constructability (settlement, density, morphology, connection with the landscape) and recovery of countryside undergoing a rapid fragmentation process. For instance, each new hub constructed must enable the creation or management of a minimum of 1 kilometre of rural roadways.

Since 2004, this project has benefited from the rapid availability of resources from the InnovationNetwork organization attached to the Ministry of the Economy, Agriculture and Innovation, in the form of a pilot project to develop rural networks. Among other things, the feasibility of a number of aspects of the project was tested. In the first instance, mobility studies showed that an increase in the number of new arrivals in the fabric of the farms did not increase the traffic generated by movement of agricultural machinery, but did induce a change in land perception and practice. The economics of the project were evaluated on the basis of a number of test sites in the local government areas of Geesteren (19 ha), Vasse (45 ha) and Tubbergen (41 ha). The cost of acquisition and preparation of the land, construction of new dwellings, and management of part of the countryside were weighed against the revenues generated by farmers from the sale of land and buildings. These first feasibility studies encouraged the province to launch other pilot projects. The first sales are scheduled for the spring of 2012.

The quality of this strategy mainly resides in characterizing the identity of the cultural landscape of the Twente region and of the specific nature of each situation. By skilfully pointing to less well known phenomena of rapid transformation in rural space, and proposing simple principles, van Paridon X de Groot have succeeded in assembling a number of valuable partners to implement the vision. While the first prototypes should provide a good test of the coherence of the project principles, their multiplication is necessary if this project is to be extended in the region. This procedure fits well with the Dutch expertise in conservation through development.

Programme Strategy for rural development **Designer** Van Paridon X de Groot **Commissioned by** Province of Overijssel, InnovatieNetwerk and Tubbergen Municipality **Design** 2003 (strategy) and 2010 (design pilot) **Implementation** 2010 onwards **Budget** not applicable

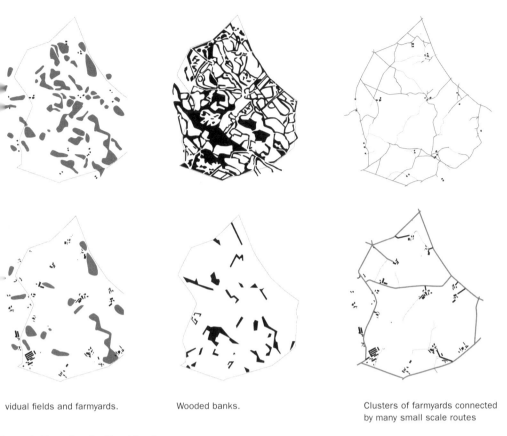

vidual fields and farmyards.

Wooded banks.

Clusters of farmyards connected
by many small scale routes

gmentation of agricultural land.
ation in 1900 (above) and in 2000.

nomous development of dairy
ns (left) and development with
farm strategy.

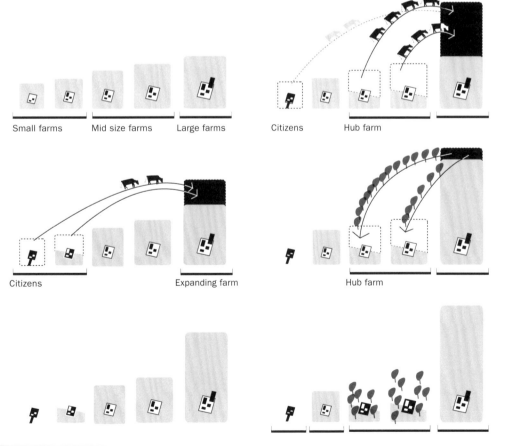

Small farms   Mid size farms   Large farms

Citizens   Hub farm

Citizens   Expanding farm

Hub farm

Range of farm types and sizes

Enriched range of farm types and sizes

All farm houses have a private side with a view of the landscape.

Front view of the hub farm including the old farm house and barn used as a garage.

inner courtyard with public paths, front doors, work spaces and barns.

w from the house to the forest lawn, which is used for grazing.

Routes connect the inner courtyard with the surrounding landscape.

Example of the hub farm designed by Franz Ziegler. Photo Harry Harsema

'Dragnet investigation' – an experiment that aims to trace the character of a region: evidence, witnesses, history and stories as indicators for development opportunities.
The town of Günne in northern South Westphalia was chosen as the centre of the dragnet area by chance because the team was provided with a suitable and beautiful workspace in the Denk-werkstatt belonging to the Montag Stiftungen, Bonn. The size of the dragnet area covered an area of 2500 km², a plausible regional scale for examining the spatial pattern of the land- and settlementscape. Each STUDIO researcher examined a 100 km² large square from the grid of the 1:50,000 topographical map. The allocation of squares was decided by drawing lots. An af-fection for an area was seen as positive and to be cultivated. A chance encounter or point of contact, be it a person, location, topographical elevation or something else, served as the start-ing point. From there, each investigator set out to explore their quadrant, stalking the neighbourhood, following leads from local residents and choosing paths to follow, changing their mode of transport at least once – with the proviso that at least 3 hours had to be undertaken on foot – until they reached Günne. The paths chosen could be arduous to travel, and cross-country routes were also permitted. Each investigator had to spend a night in their quadrant. During the investigation, each researcher recorded their findings, noting down conversations had or over-heard, sounds and smells. They drew, measured, took samples, dug, filmed and photographed. Immersion without an explicit agenda is important, as if travelling with no particular destina-tion, willing to see what turns up and what happens: lingering for a while, assuming roles, being boundless, becoming one with the space in which one is; in short, inviting what Hinderk Emrich has described as 'participation mystique'.
Once in Günne the investigators created the entire area as a multi-dimensional pictorial representation made of sticky tape and newspaper, designing as they built it. In the process, a new poetic 'landscape name' was found for the region. Sitting some-times for long periods in front of their newly created model of the region, the investigators searched for meaning, attempting to understand what it tells them, how it affects them, what con-tact they have to the region – perhaps through metaphors? or topography? or people? whether visions are already manifesting themselves? They began to mark the first layers on the model, to sketch and discuss, to go for walks, to write …

Earth and sky and the ability to recognize the relationships that occur on, within or between them as being interconnected is what characterizes looking from the viewpoint of landscape.

TOWARDS CREATIVE KNOWLEDGE

According to the American philosopher Nelson Goodman, 'Recognizing patterns is very much a matter of inventing and imposing them. Comprehension and creation go on together.' Design as a creative activity for the space-oriented disciplines[1] entails being able to comprehend regions as landscapes, to develop ideas for developmental processes for the entire region, for (individual) projects and initiatives, a strategy for their implementation, a communication concept that unites as many participants as possible as well as having a plausible line of argumentation. In this context, designing is a specific mode of cognition, one that can be considered as a "sitting on the fence" mode of science, planning, everyday practice and art in addition to the theoretical and space-oriented claims of the different disciplines: all of which are 'Mode 2 sciences' as defined by Helga Nowotny. It is only through this crossover that design is able to adequately address the complexity and dynamism of what we call *Raumgeschehen*, that is of spatial activities in all their dimensions. Depending on the context of the task at hand, design can lean more towards science or towards practice.

DESIGNING IS INTEGRATIVE. Creative cognition – which we describe as *understanding* in our book *Creating Knowledge* – therefore plays a key role: 'In the STUDIO URBANE LAND-SCHAFTEN our specific approach to looking at space is through landscape (as the overarching perspective). What we mean is that we see *landscape* as *one* possible means of understanding space. This means not only that natural conditions and nature processes are considered alongside and on an equal footing with human and man-made processes, but also that we abandon the categories of *natural* and *artificial*. By considering space from the viewpoint of landscape, we stress both the way in which landscape is perceived as a *whole* that integrates many aspects yet is still not clearly definable, as well as the fundamentally positive connotation of landscape. [...] We discuss *designing as an integrative process of creating knowledge*. Cognition and the creation of knowledge are always understood as process and result, but in general a differentiation is made between intuitive and discursive cognition. We are interested in the synthesis of both threads of cognition.' Our approach addresses in many respects the present notion of design at a regional scale as a future-oriented means of cognition that brings together research and practice and is able to respond to the complexity of contemporary development issues. In most cases, a design will evolve at three levels: an overarching level that concerns the spatial activities or *Raumgeschehen* as a whole, the level of the individual design measures and between them a level of strategic communication that is concerned with the space in question, the progress of discussions, the design, communications, strategy and implementation.[2]

essay reflects ongoing
ourse and collaboration
ong the STUDIO members
he topic and its theoreti-
examination in disserta-
s. (Lucia Grosse Bächle on
ess: 'Eine Pflanze ist kein
n', Hanover 2003; Margit
ld on transitoriness: 'Disap-
rance. Temporary installa-
s in landscape and open
ce planning. A contribution
urrent discourse', Hanover
5; Daniela Karow-Kluge on
eriments: 'Experiments in
public realm', Berlin 2010;
a Werner on the first steps
esign approaches; Henrik
ultz on walking as a method
reating knowledge; Sigrun
gner on mapping; Christiane
ia on playing). It is informed
he STUDIO's international
m for doctorate students
hich these themes are
subject of ongoing and
troversial examination and
ussion. It likewise reflects
earch activities in the
DIO context and a larger
nber of projects undertaken
arious offices whose work-
methods share a more or
s similar approach, as well
a large number of student
ects in which the design
roach has been developed,
ed and put into action.
ally, the essay draws on
cles published as part of
ating Knowledge. Innovation
ategies for Designing Urban
dscapes, Berlin 2008.

Space-oriented disciplines
considered here as a
le although discourse on
e-scale regional develop-
nt and design as research
tinues to take place largely
ependently of one another,
evidenced most recently by
eikones NCCR iconic criti-
n conference wissenschaft
werfen. Vom forschenden
werfen zur Entwurfsforsc-
g der Architektur (Designing
ence. From investigative
ign to design research in ar-
ecture) in November 2011.

The three levels are not en-
ly identical to Andrea Kahn's
as of effect, areas of impact
l areas of experiment, but
bear relation to them – an
resting discussion in its
n right.

The term 'models' as used
e does not mean the gener-
applicable model as used
atural sciences.

THE FIRST LEVEL: UNDERSTANDING RAUMGESCHEHEN AS A WHOLE. *Creating a line of inquiry and its relevant space.*

In many cases a design task or competition brief will prescribe the issues to be adressed and the space concerned. In such cases, it can be productive to reformulate the question and the task at hand, and to re-examine the extent of the relevant space. In many other cases, an issue may be invented to start with, based on a current level of knowledge, and a client then sought – an approach that is perhaps somewhat unusual in landscape architecture and town and regional planning. In the example cited at the beginning, issues and initial ideas are sought by experimental means, drawing on the interdisciplinary group's expertise and knowledge of the problems of sparsely populated regions in Germany. In the *Wadden Coast landscape vision*, published in this book and entitled *Go with the Flow*, it remains unclear who formulated the task and who will put it into action – possibly because the article on the project is so short? In the *Hub Farms* project, a region was first chosen for the master studies thesis project and a strategic approach then 'derived' from the agricultural dynamics of the region and its effect on the small farming producers. In principle this 'inventive' or 'creative' approach to discovering issues and formulating tasks is inherent to many design approaches at a regional scale and amounts in effect to one of the productive alliances between research and design.

Experimental investigation and the idea. As described in the 'Dragnet Investigation', understanding a space means to probe and grasp the complexity of a space in its entirety, intuitively, emotionally and with the senses. In the Dragnet experiment, a large and diverse area is explored in a idea-generating way using structured random sampling methods borrowed and adapted from other disciplines – such as grid sampling, probing, combing, walking, wandering, random scatter points, chance encounters, following given directions etc. – and the subdivision into grid quadrants, as commonly used in geography, pedology or geology. This is combined with a direct approach to exploring space physically that emphatically embraces the things and occurrences stumbled upon in a random and non-exhaustive manner as one moves through and spends contemplative time in the space in question. It is driven by a desire to understand everything about the space while simultaneously acknowledging the impossibility of doing so: this is what dragnet investigation is about – what Bernard Lassus describes as persuading reality to reveal itself.

Pictorial expression and ideas. The entire space is described in the form of a picture, sketch, model or poem in its current manifestation and simultaneously in its hypothetical development, and in the process the space is given a (new) name. The result is informed by the different backgrounds and experiences of the team members. In the case of the 'Dragnet Investigation', the image is a three-dimensional model. As Alfred North Whitehead has noted in the past, it is through aesthetic-creative ability that it becomes possible to perceive and express such complex relationships intuitively. The uncertain nature of the pictorial representation leaves room for interpretation: no attempt is made to reduce complexity but rather to work with it. An important aspect of this kind of image is that it functions as a means of transformation: it tells stories from the present but, due to its interpretative character, also embodies the future. That is often hard to communicate, but the process of analysis is also creative. In the context of scientific work, such pictorial representations function almost as qualitative models[3] – or sometimes as dynamic landscape machines[4] or sequences of images. The representation makes concrete references to the qualities of the space in question, without being a straightforward reproduction or visualization of the space but also without eradicating its specific qualities, as abstracted models sometimes do through their tendency to generalize. For example, the title 'Small scale sand landscapes in Overijssel' embodies both the task as well as the idea in the name of the landscape. The unfolding series of sketches in the *Wadden Coast Landscape Vision* function as pictures, while the before-and-after maps produced in the *Hub Farms* project are perhaps overly cartographic rather than pictorial. It is clear, though, that a picture can appear at the beginning, at the end or as an evolving processual picture.

THE SECOND LEVEL: STRATEGIC COMMUNICATION. *Stories.* The character of the space is retold from the perspective of the idea[5] (i.e. the plot) through maps, layers, images, diagrams, statistics, mapping, models, new systems of relationships, patterns of dynamics, through types or portraits of people, principles or metaphors.[6] In our Dragnet example, the first set of relationships are marked on the model. The *Hub Farms* project consists of clear maps that show a historical comparison of key landscape characteristics in the project area and the changes they have undergone. Accompanying photos illustrate the beauty of the intended principles. Other projects show more complex representations of dynamic changes as, for example, demonstrated by James Corner in his pioneering work for Fresh Kills Park in 2005.

Prognostic frame. In the design of large-scale areas, research and planning enter into an alliance, formulating plausible hypotheses for the future as a prognostic frame. From these, more precise issues and problems can be formulated. The *Wadden Coast Landscape Vision* and the *Hub Farms* project illustrate this principle: the landscape vision reveals the problems caused by current planning strategies by showing the rising tides, the unattractive mud flats of the coastline, the raising of the dikes,

The term 'models' as used
e does not mean the gener-
applicable model as used
atural sciences.

For example, in the form of
uilt landscape machine as
he 'Im Stromland' student
ect, Hanover 2010 by
a Schultz u.a (mentors:
e Stokam, Sabine Rabe)
as a metaphor as used by
run Langner: 'Landschafts-
schine. Landschaftsproduz-
nde Kräfte im Ruhrgebiet'
Christa Reicher, Klaus R.
zmann, Jan Polívka, Frank
st, Yasemin Utku, Michael
gener (Ed.): Schichten
er Region – Kartenstücke zur
mlichen Struktur des Ruhrge-
ts, 2011, pp. 132-157.

Julia Werner asserts that
as are deciphering aids
t are crucial to navigating
mplex problems. See 'Ideas
ow can they emerge?' in:
ating Knowledge, 2008, p.
0/301.

The dangers and participa-
y challenges inherent in
rocess that relies on a
sign-oriented interpretational
proach are discussed by
ga Nowotny and Giuseppe
sta in the context of different
entific disciplines in their
ok Naked Genes: Reinvent-
the Human in the Molecular
e, MIT 2011.

Reflection is, of course, a
damental part of research
ctice just as it is for sci-
ce: another alliance. Stories,
wever, don't necessarily
e to be 'if-then' construc-
ns; they need to capture the
tingency of the situation
d embody an element of
xplicability.

Future scenarios can take
ny forms, for example maps
the Altes Land project,
ematic sections in the
sseratlas project, or layers in
e Fresh Kills Park project.

Our research fol-
ved Wasseratlas as a
search-practice project,
en a dialogical laboratory, a
actice-report project entitled
eelbekonzep', a cooperative,
nciples-in-practice design
ject entitled Deichpark, the
ichbude, a practical imple-
entation as acupuncture,
eetsand as a practice model
ject, a further dialogical
oratory and then a return to
search using the Deichpark
amples as model projects for
esearch project.

the severed relationship between localities and the sea, the land reclamation efforts and concomitant sinking of land levels and the problem of drinking water production. The *Hub Farms* project links the changes in agricultural structures that are leading to the destruction of small-scale landscape structures with the search for good living conditions.

Plot, story, principles, experiments. The design process as a dynamic strategy – in both research and practice – needs to follow a plausible rationale[7]. Participants need to be found, as do instruments, money and effective means of intervention. The principle of the plot is necessary for the story to function. The plot also incorporates emotions. The plot of the *Wadden Coast landscape vision* lies in linking together disparate areas: flood protection, drinking water production and landscape qualities. The plot of the *Hub Farms* project lies in the establishment of a kind of agency (the precise form is not made clear in the article) that aims to create a win-win strategy by matching the remaining leftover pieces of former agricultural land with interested actors – in this case househunters – in order to invest the landscape with new landscape qualities.

Future scenarios. The future is to be shaped through sections, spatial areas, networks, structures, layers or actions and argumentation. One example is the small sectional drawings in the *Wadden Coast Landscape Vision*; another is the creation of test designs. Such future scenarios are always backed up by references – such as citations as a kind of 'proof' of their feasibility and compatibility.[8]

Dialogue. The design of large-scale areas requires dialogue processes, which Ursula Stein describes as a 'learning method'. These dialogues concern re-connecting and exchanging information, references and citations, argumentation and verification and the involvement of actors and stakeholders. But dialogues also need to be imbued with a design aesthetic! That way they can appeal to the senses and emotions and cultivate enthusiasm, increasing their chance of success. From a methodological standpoint, dialogues with laypeople and different kinds of experts can help objectify the design.

THE THIRD LEVEL: INDIVIDUAL MEASURES. *Interventions and verification.* During the process, the first concrete steps can already be put into action to act as initial impulses. These can be temporary initiatives such as exhibitions or events that aim to raise awareness or alter perceptions. They share a basic principle: they should be small interventions with maximum effect. They must be designed, planned and put into action, along with a corresponding means of measuring responses. Their effect can be measured in laboratory discussions or workshops, ex-

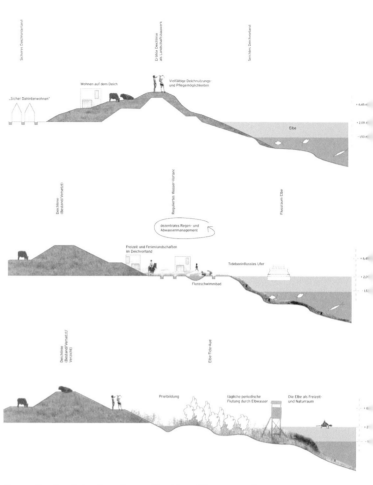

FIRST LEVEL. Above: The topological image of Water-Land Elbe Island (52 km²) reveals the relationship between the topography and tidal changes as they happen, and as an instrument of action for the future. Right: 3x3 scenarios derived from the topological study, in which three different spatial aspects have been tested according to three different action principles.

Source: Wasseratlas. STUDIO URBANE LANDSCHAFTEN.
In: IBA Hamburg (HG.), *Wasseratlas. WasserLand-Topologien für die Hamburger Elbinsel.* Hamburg 2008.

Example of a dyke foreshore situation: The scenarios combine the following spatial characters and action principles: 1) foreshore and land regulation, 2) protected land and land reclamation, 3) marshland and land dynamisation.

SECOND LEVEL. Dyke Park Elbe Island (sketch above) and Dyke Park exhibition (right): the mediation project and ideas workshop facilitated the process of reinterpreting the flood control requirements into principles for landscape design. The WaterLand Elbe Island image (left) served as an underlying design principle. Encircled by a 27km long dyke, its foreshore and hinterland have been designated as parkland. The exhibition was inspired by the park metaphor, and was used to communicate about the why, how, who and where of the project.

Source: Deichpark. osp urbanelandschaften, Hamburg.
In: IBA Hamburg: *Deichpark Elbinsel* 2011 and *Deichpark Ausstellung.* osp urbanelandschaften, Hamburg.

RD LEVEL. Existing tidal outlets have been trans-
med into huts with an exhibition space, a hotel, a
-watching tower and other places of interest. The
eased visibililty helps raise awareness about the
l changes of the River Elbe.

e huts and exhibition: osp urbanelandschaften with Thomas
el, since 2010.

References

[1] Hinderk Emrich: *Was Engel und Avatare uns sagen können*. Lecture in Landow, Germany on 13 June 2010 (unpublished). 'Participation mystique' as a condition akin to the blankness before the divine spark (Arthur Köstler) or Husserl's concept of epoché or 'bracketing' which denotes an ability to stay aware, understand and suspend judgement. See also Peter Sloterdijk: *Scheintod im Denken, Von Philosophie und Wissenschaft als Übung*, 2010 pp. 60-98 (Suspended in Thought – On Philosophy and Science as Practice, English edition forthcoming) and Byung-Chul Han: *Der Duft der Zeit*, 2009.

[2] Nelson Goodman, *Ways of Worldmaking*, 1978.

[3] Helga Nowotny, Peter Scott, Michael Gibbens, *Re-Thinking Science: Knowledge and the Public in an Age of Uncertainty*, 2001.

[4] Hille von Seggern, 'Understanding is Essential for Designing', in Hille von Seggern, Julia Werner, Lucia Grosse-Bächle (Ed) *Creating Knowledge. Innovation Strategies for Designing Urban Landscapes*, 2008, pp. 212-251.

[5] Jean Grondin, 'Gadamer's Basic Understanding of Understanding', in Robert J.Dostal (Ed.) *The Cambridge Companion to Gadamer*, 2002.

[6] Hille von Seggern, Julia Werner, 'Designing as an Integrative Process of Creating Knowledge', in *Creating Knowledge. Innovation Strategies for Designing Urban Landscapes*, 2008, p. 55 and p. 39.

[7] Brigitte Franzen, Stefanie Krebs, *Landschaftstheorie. Texte der Cultural Landscape*, 2005.

[8] Jürgen von Reuß, 'Lassus in Kassel – Ein Blick auf die Gartenkunst', in Andrea Koenecke, Udo Weilacher, Joachim Wolschke-Buhlmann (Ed). *Die Kunst, Landschaft neu zu erfinden. Werk und Wirken von Bernard Lassus*, 2010, p. 92.

[9] Alfred North Whitehead, *Modes of Thought*, 1968.

[10] James Corner, 'Lifescape – Fresh Kills Parkland' among others in *Topos* 51/2005, pp. 14-21.

[11] Ursula Stein, *Lernende Stadtregion. Verständigungsprozesse über Zwischenstadt*, 2006.

[12] Martin Prominski, *Landschaftsentwerfen*, 2003, p. 116 and p. 105.

[13] Helga Nowotny, 'Design as a working knowledge', in *Creating Knowledge*, 2008, pp. 12-15.

pert panel discussions or simply through observation (extensive scientific monitoring is not necessary). The *Hub Farms* project is exemplary in this respect in that it presents initial projects. Whether the effect these have as experiments is actually monitored is not discussed in the article.

Line of argumentation and implementation. Such processes are not finished when a report is finalized or a design is handed over. Their strategic, long-term character necessitates a structured procedure for the future course of action that details its implementation and is backed up by a plausible line of argumentation. This can entail shifts between the fields of activity: from practice back to research and vice versa[9]. The design of large-scale areas does not come to a conclusion once it has been ratified as part of a binding plan or published in a book: it is always oriented towards direct action.

DESIGN AS A SCIENTIFIC ACTIVITY. If we are to speak of designing as a process of cognition, of creating knowledge, we must also consider the question of how scientific the process of design is, a notion that is met with great scepticism in the academic realm. The process of designing has been researched in terms of its techniques and in its applications of systemic, algorithmic, constructive or aesthetic dimensions, but design as a means of research, as a specific 'working knowledge' as Helga Nowotny has called it, has not yet joined the ranks of the "indispensible plants in the garden of knowledge production" as Martin Prominski has rightly demanded. It is time to call into question the universal appropriateness of scientific or engineering-led comprehension and to recognize the independent cognitive contribution of design. Prominski has taken a significant step in this direction by attributing design to the so-called Mode 2 sciences, as described by Nowotny et al. In contrast to the causal knowledge production of Mode 1 sciences, Mode 2 describes knowledge that is typically contextual or relational, that is inseparable from society, economics or culture and often the product of trans-disciplinary inquiry. As such, the discussion is not about either-ors but rather the need to extend the canon of sciences that deal with the complexities of the real world.

Put another way, research can benefit from the knowledge, means of cognition and tools of design – and design in turn from the knowledge, means of cognition and methods of science. And both stand to benefit from considering intuition, sensibility and physical response alongside rational reasoning. This is the basis we need in order to bring about dynamic possibilities which in their manifestation have the capacity to touch us as human beings, vitally improving our lives by offering adequate responses to the complexities of the real world.

Dr. Hille von Seggern (architect, urban planner, open space planner) founded STUDIO URBANE LANDSCHAFTEN in 2005 together with Julia Werner and in 2008 became a senior advisor to osp urbanelandschaften in Hamburg. Until 2008, von Seggern was professor of landscape design and urban development at the Leibniz University Hanover. She has worked together with Timm Ohrt

WADDEN COAST LANDSCAPE VISION
designed by Buro Harro

The new salt marshland, an almost disappeared Wadden landscape, acts as a bufferzone for high tides.

In some parts of Europe landscape design is used to investigate urgent social issues. In the Dutch province of Friesland landscape architecture is contributing to the search for solutions to the problems caused by the rising level of the Wadden Sea. In contrast to traditional civil engineering solutions – such as raising the dyke level – this design approach involves linking up with other sorts of problems. In the Climate Change Friesland project coastal defence is not the only objective; the idea is to imbue the relatively unattractive Wadden coast with new meaning. This will include ecological features, opportunities for water storage further inland, potential for tourism and restoring the spatial relations between the towns of Friesland and the sea. Buro Harro, based in Arnhem, has developed a vision in which the hard, raised edge of the Friesland coastline will become a broad, dynamic zone. Land outside the dykes will once again need to be reclaimed, not for agricultural purposes but to create extensive areas of salt marsh. These typical Wadden landscapes, which have almost disappeared, act as a buffer zone for high tides. In Buro Harro's vision, a system of piers and attractions – such as a big hollow *terp*, or mound, with room for a campsite, and a former drilling platform – will create access. Within this outstanding overall concept, only the formalization hasn't completely convinced the jury: the pattern of paths doesn't seem to fit in with the wild and unpredictable environment of the salty marshlands. [mh]

Programme Long-term vision for the Frisian Wadden coast **Designer** Buro Harro (Harro de Jong) **In collaboration with** Royal Haskoning (Martin Groenewoud) **Commissioned by** Atelier Fryslân **Area** 5000 km² **Design** 2009 **Budget** not applicable

The overall concept: the hard, raised edge of the Friesland coastline will become a broad, dynamic zone once again.

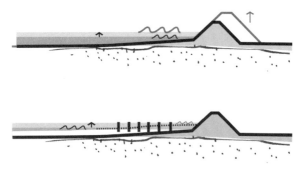

Dykes need to be raised to cope with the rising sea level (above). Creating salt marshes will do away with the need to strengthen the dykes.

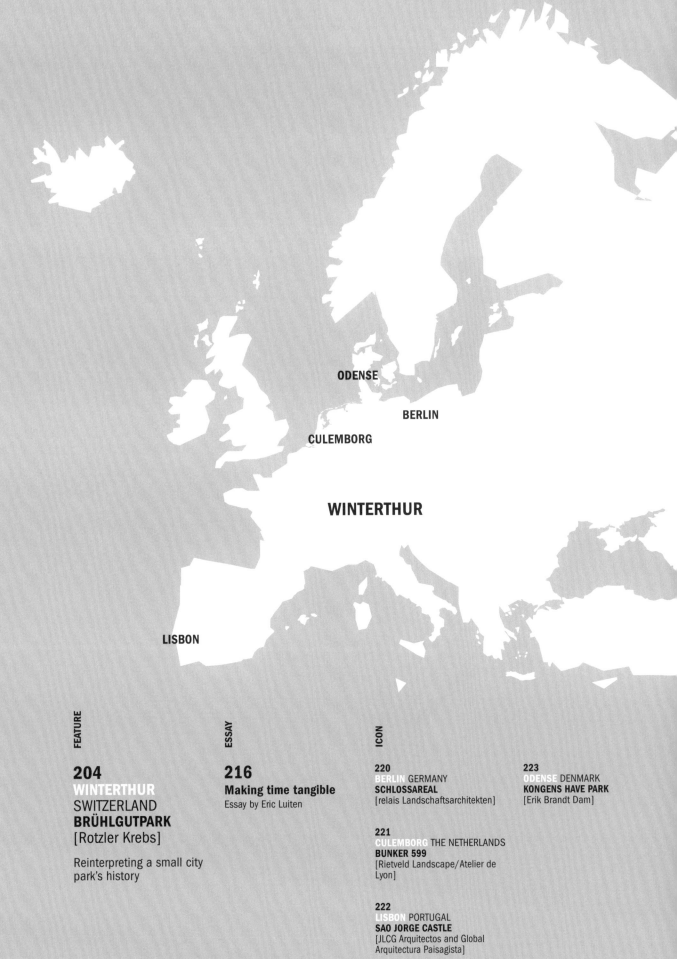

DESIGN WITH HISTORY

ODENSE

BERLIN

CULEMBORG

WINTERTHUR

LISBON

FEATURE

204
WINTERTHUR
SWITZERLAND
BRÜHLGUTPARK
[Rotzler Krebs]

Reinterpreting a small city
park's history

ESSAY

216
Making time tangible
Essay by Eric Luiten

ICON

220
BERLIN GERMANY
SCHLOSSAREAL
[relais Landschaftsarchitekten]

221
CULEMBORG THE NETHERLANDS
BUNKER 599
[Rietveld Landscape/Atelier de
Lyon]

222
LISBON PORTUGAL
SAO JORGE CASTLE
[JLCG Arquitectos and Global
Arquitectura Paisagista]

223
ODENSE DENMARK
KONGENS HAVE PARK
[Erik Brandt Dam]

The trees of the English landscaped garden have been integrated in the redesigned park. All photos Christian Schwager

BRÜHLGUTPARK

designed by Rotzler Krebs Partner

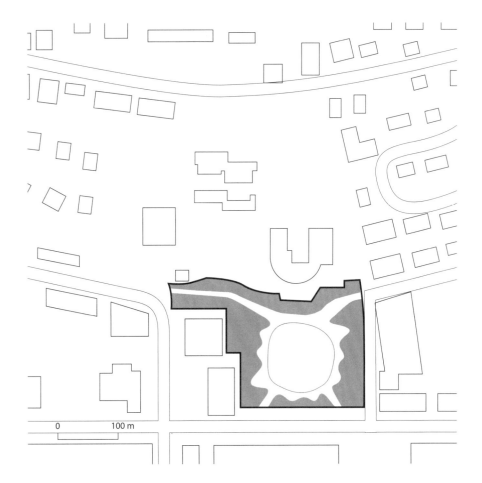

0   100 m

JURY COMMENT Like many historical city parks in Europe, Brühlgutpark has had a career of its own. One might even call it a biography: from a grand landscaped garden, to a prim public area, to a popular district park that seemed to be going to rack and ruin in the recent past. It is impressive to see how meticulously yet sensitively the landscape architects analysed the park's historical layout, respectfully paid tribute to its history, and in that way devised a new, complex spatial structure for our times. Instead of all-encompassing interventions, the landscape architects have created a new framework in a simple language that is nonetheless highly sophisticated in its subtlety: 'Landscape is about transformation through time and people.'

Project plan.

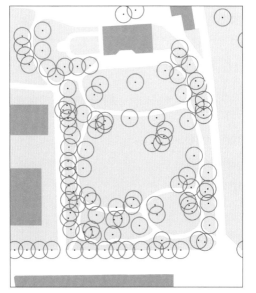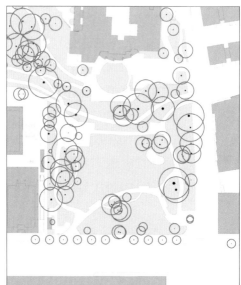

From neoclassical landscaped park to versatile city park.

Reinterpreting a small city park's history

Feature by Claudia Moll

The most conspicuous feature of the new Brühlgutpark is the grey concrete strip. Enclosing the central greenery, its function changes with its height: at ground level, it invites pedestrians to walk on it. Slightly higher, it is a seating element. Further along its course, it encourages skipping and play. Young children whizz around it,circling on their balance bikes; seniors out with their walking frames use it as a sporting challenge; at lunchtime, it offers plenty of space to sit and enjoy a break from work, and when it gets dark, teens and couples like to congregate here. The strip nestles into the surrounding terrain and is a highlight in this small park in the Winterthur district of Tössfeld.

The credit goes to the landscape architects Rotzler Krebs Partner. Emerging as the winners of a selection process in 2006, they fundamentally redesigned the former neoclassical landscape garden with a few well-chosen interventions. While engaging with the place's history, they very soon actively rejected the idea of reconstructing the park, opting instead to create a contemporary public park with the emphasis on re-interpretation rather than historic conservation.

Brühlgutpark is part of a grand landscaped park built at the end of the 19th century. It was commissioned by the Rieter-Ziegler family of industrialists on the grounds of their villa at the foot of Brühlberg hill by the renowned landscape garden architect Conrad Löwe (1819–1870). The villa and park were located in the immediate vicinity of expanding factories and new workers' estates in the small town to the north of Zürich, which developed into an important location of industry in the course of the 19th century. When the municipality of Winterthur purchased the property in 1920 and set up a municipal old people's home in the villa, the section of the park between the house and Zürcherstrasse road became the public facility known as Brühlgutanlage (Brühlgut Park). In 1948, the landscape architect Gustav Ammann adapted it to meet new needs. He did so by replacing the winding paths of the landscape garden with a functional network of routes interspersed with small open areas, paved with polygonal paving stones. As the years went by, the park became the green centre of an increasingly densely built district. The municipal authorities embellished it as they saw fit and to meet requirements, adding a children's playground, cycle paths, seating and streetlamps. The villa was eventually demolished in 1983 and a new old people's home was built instead. From that moment onward, a round eight-storey high brick building overlooked the green area, but the terrace to the front no longer afforded direct access to the park. Traffic on the adjoining Zürcherstrasse increased steadily. Noise and exhaust fumes deterred visitors more and more. The district park was increasingly beset by problems associated with littering, drug use and vandalism and threatened to turn into a slum. The locals wanted their park back and demanded a redesign. Municipal authorities reacted in 2006 by requesting selected agencies to submit designs. The contract was awarded to Rotzler Krebs Partner Landschaftsarchitekten. The brief was a new focal point for the district, whose industrial areas had long since become derelict and which was subject to increasing densification following the construction of residential and service buildings.

Comparison of old plans with contemporary aerial photographs soon showed the landscape architects that little remained of the picturesque 19th century landscaped gardens apart from a few stately clusters of trees. This prompted them to opt for a spatial re-interpretation that would respect the location's history while meeting the manifold requirements of a city park of our times.

The focal point of the new Brühlgutpark is the open area of greenery mentioned at the start, which is encircled by the *Beton-Collier* (Concrete Necklace). This is bordered in turn by a path spread with red sand. Its undulating outer margin gives rise to indentations which, equipped with seating or playground equipment, are an inviting place to spend time. Trees more than a century old, growing by the path and on the round lawn, cast light, airy shade. Densely planted areas on the park's edge contrast with the open central area. Newly planted trees and shrubs complement the existing woody plants on the longitudinal sides and create a lively backdrop. Whereas the character in these areas is predominantly darker and forest-like – evergreen oleaster, holly, boxwood shrubs and woody perennials frame the space – the transverse sides of the grassy area are planted with profuse beds of herbaceous perennials. The 'flower window' mainly composed of blue-flowering plants lies below the terrace fronting the old people's home and gives a pleasant view from there. The 'carpet of perennials' in various yellows along the Zürcherstrasse pavement draws the eye of passers-by. The fence behind the park is a playful re-interpretation of the picket fence that used to stand here. The steel tubes set in the preserved natural stone base wall compose a shimmering curtain that shelters park visitors from Zürcherstrasse.

The landscape architects focused their design efforts on the concrete strip and the fence, drawing inspiration from the works of contemporary artists. The Concrete Necklace was inspired by Distorted Circle with a Polygon by the American minimalist Robert Mangold: an oval drawn on an orange-yellow polygonal area, squashed at the margins and slightly dented. The concrete strip was to fit into Brühlgutpark in exactly the same way. Its shape accommodates the roots of the existing trees and forms a connection between the raised areas of land in the existing terrain. The landscape architects did not see the latter as a hindrance but as the starting point for a subtle play on the different levels. Since the unique geometry of the ensuing strip made prefabrication impossible, the planners had it cast in sections on-site in a flexible mould, emphasizing its sculptural expression with rounded edges and a sandblasted surface. Taking up the theme of speed and motion, the Dancing Fence was erected alongside Zürcherstrasse. The inspirational force in this instance was the works of op art artist Victor Vasarely, whose abstract spatial patterns create disconcerting optical effects for the viewer. The landscape architects applied this principle to the almost three-metre-high boundary: prefabricated steel tubes with exactly the same curvature were mounted on iron bases in varying degrees of rotation. As a result, the fence appears to dance depending on the speed at which it is passed.

Apart from these two design highlights and the abundant plantings, the 'side shows' are impressive too: the playground is not cut off from the rest of the park, but interwoven with trees and shrubs to create a climbing forest; the lighting bathes the paths in a pleasant light and a new, carefully designed set of steps leads to the ter-

race of the old people's home. New railings transform the latter to a belvedere with a wide view over the park. The individual interventions are adaptations tailored by the landscape architects to meet the varying requirements in the specific locations.

The partner in charge of the project, Matthias Krebs, said the generous time budget available was a luxury that contributed to the successful planning and construction process. The planners had three whole years to explore various options and had the freedom to allow their ideas to 'settle' and develop further. One reason was because the construction project owners saw the park as a driver of social development: they hoped it would give the sadly dilapidated district a new centre and a new lease of life. The head of the municipal plant nursery, Christian Wieland, acted as advocate for the planners' ideas and expedited their passage through all of the committees and authorities involved. The willingness of the municipal plant nursery to do the substantial upkeep and maintenance work required is at the same time an important sign of commitment to the continuation of the facility.

Programme Redesigning Brühlgutpark Designer Rotzler Krebs Partner Landscape Architects (Matthias Krebs, Alexander Heinrich, Stefan Rotzler, Eva Dorsch, Sabine Kanne, Andreas Haustein, Achim Schefer, Manon Büttiker) In collaboration with Civil engineers: Dr Deuring + Oehninger AG; lighting designers: art Light; surveyors: U. Müller Ingenieure Commissioned by Winterthur municipality, represented by Winterthur Stadtgärtnerei (municipal plant nursery) Area 0.83 ha Design Study commission 2006; project 2007–2009 Implementation 2009/2010 Budget €1,653,000 (construction)

The park before redesign. Photo RKP

rge path spread with red sand borders the green centre.

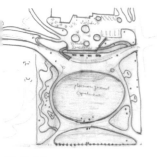

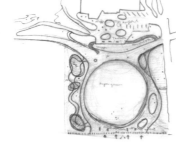

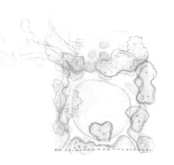

Robert Mangold, Distorted Circle Within a Polygon (1972).

aft sketches.

Carefully designed steps link the terrace of the old people's home with the park.

A Dancing Fence of curved steel tubes forms a border between the park and the street.

The children's playground is shaded by old trees.

ellow-blossomed perennials predominate in the flowerbed along the fence.

The Concrete Necklace and central lawn are used in many ways.

MAKING TIME TANGIBLE

Essay by Eric Luiten

More than in the 20th century, in the coming decades we will be confronted with the spatial challenges of breathing new life into existing artefacts, structures and landscapes. We have emerged from a post-war phase of new construction, expansion and development, one where we hardly needed to worry about what was already there. We had institutional mechanisms and tactics to be able to select what was considered worthy of survival as cultural heritage. This chosen historical material could be included and safeguarded in the rapidly growing collection of listed and preserved monuments and protected cultural landscapes. As a result, a part of the physical environment was isolated and exempted from an area's spatial dynamics. That which was not highly valued could be demolished or drastically adapted to new requirements. But the balance between preservation and renewal has today taken a different turn: the stabilizing demographics and the economic uncertainties that are currently affecting Europe, call for a different relationship between society and the historic environment. Designers and planners have to thoroughly prepare for the question of how the historic city and the historic landscape will have to adapt to changing social expectations and programmes. How can the huge stock of existing houses, shops, churches, barracks, convents, offices and factories, and the vast expanses of agricultural lands and farms be reused or redesigned in flexible and sustainable ways? The commissioning of projects for the physical environment will undergo a gradual shift of focus from that which is new to that which is already there.

This trend of reusing structures and spaces in our physical environment must be handled with delicacy because that which already exists in a socio-psychological sense holds collective meaning and therefore value. People feel attached to their living environment, regardless of whether heritage professionals have attributed to it historical or other qualities. Histories and remembrances, individual and collective memory, they are all supported and reinforced by objects and patterns in the city and the countryside. This means that preparations for physical interventions in the city, village or neighbourhood require architects and spatial designers who are sincerely interested in the complex relationship that people maintain with their familiar surroundings. Designers will need to, more than ever, ask themselves what position they want to take in relation to their own professional background and repertoire, and in relation to the history of the location. Our experience from studies of landscape architectural adaptations of old patterns and struc-

3. Cito, 'Geschiedenis
etterlijk fundament', in
verpen aan Geschiedenis
agazine Drie, Stimulerings-
s Architectuur Rotterdam
tory as Literal Founda-
, in Designing with History
agazine 3, Netherlands
iitecture Fund), 2005.

tures is that there are difficulties in articulating major themes such as history, nostalgia and heritage in the designed interventions. Designers generally deal with this question in a very pragmatic and often opportunistic way. They tend to rationalize their work in popular or even mystifying terms when describing what they envisioned or were trying to achieve with their proposed transformation. This makes any discussion about possible changes to a particular historic site or monument very difficult or at least unsatisfactory. Clients are often unable to formulate carefully enough the limits to which planned interventions may be visible or perceived, or how the future design itself should relate to the qualities of the existing historic design. There is great need for a conceptual framework within which a proper dialogue can take place between designer and object, and between designer and society, on possible transformations of our heritage landscapes.

To begin with, it is important to re-examine the relationship between the historian and the designer. In the ideal situation, a historical site that must be adapted or transformed should first be subjected to historical research. Historical geographers and architectural historians are capable of tracing the origin and describing the subsequent fate of a specific terrain or area. They relate the site to similar ones elsewhere, they investigate the owners, users and designers of the past, and they couple it with its stories and memories. Special features are expressed in terms of integrity, rarity and representativeness, and based on such criteria the terrain or area is awarded a certain degree of historical value. By placing the site in a landscape architectural tradition or within a regional historical narrative, it becomes in a sense dematerialized. This is one reason why planners often find it difficult to work with historical research: it does not provide material support, only a temporal context and a proposition of value. The designer is – unlike the historian – not so much looking for historical definition and taxonomy, but for references or precedents for site-specific interventions that will lead to an overall appreciation and increase in value. Moreover, historians, by the very nature of their profession, are obsessed by completeness: good historical research is the most complete historical research possible. Rarely is there an attempt to distil historical references of primary or secondary importance, since history as seen by historians, knows only layering and sequences and never hierarchy. Yet this distillation is precisely what the designer needs in order to make a proposal which goes beyond simple repair or restoration. Only through making a selection of certain cultural essentials in order to highlight or even exaggerate them, can improvements take form, whether it be to an object or an area which will be getting a new function or being brought back into spatial and social circulation.

These essentials, which for the designers are of such crucial importance, can relate to the material level, to the morphological level or the semantic level. An intervention that builds on the material aspect of the heritage can be based on, for instance, a strategy of excavation, partial conservation, labelling or superposition. By using abstractions, distortions or stylizations, the viewer's attention can be drawn from the material and be led towards the morphological characteristics. References can be made to certain forms which were lost in the past, by re-introducing them in new incarnations: replicas and reconstructions, for example, become morphological interventions. At the semantic level, however, an intervention transcends the material or morphological connection and seeks to associate with the origin of the heritage, its operational or social significance. In such cases, the designer is expected to create an interpretation or a new narrative that in the majority of cases leads, after in-depth consideration, to a delayed understanding and appreciation of the object. Landscape or architectural changes of this category can be indicated by such stylistic means of expression as hyperbole, repetition or irony.

The *Bunker 599* project, designed by landscape architect Ronald Rietveld and artist Erick de Lyon, adds in a rigorous way meaning at the material level through an intervention in the physical dimension. The cut in the bunker is actually a model of the overall preservation and revitalization plan of the former New Dutch Waterline, a 19th century military defence line extending for 85 km through central Netherlands. The defence line includes a vast collection of military artefacts and ingenious waterworks, of which the bunker is one of them. The master plan for the Waterline aims to reveal and make public this previously inaccessible collection. Bunker 599 shows that the ambition of openness has basically unlocked the secrets of this military architecture and essentially nullified it. The recreational path cuts through the concrete monolith in a tasteful way and has turned its interior into an exterior. The project builds on work from a few years earlier by architect Gianni Cito for the same Waterline bunkers in which, through a series of sketches, he suggested the bunkers be developed as a literal foundation for understanding the beauty and the logic of this defence landscape.[1]

The artefacts constructed among the ruins of the *São Jorge Castle* in Lisbon, and on the former *Schlossareal* in Berlin, make use of additions which are distinct from the historical backgrounds of the sites. In Lisbon, one can speak of an ancient, layered archaeological site which the designers first lined and stabilized by means of vertical steel plates. Then the location was further partitioned and made accessible with additional layers of stone and sand at different levels, and with the construction of neutral, timeless cubicles. The landscape architectural intervention is primarily physical in nature and enhances the understanding of the history of the place. At the *Schlossareal*, a similar tactic was used to liberate a historic site without physically affecting it. A wooden boardwalk marks the original long facades of the former *Schlossareal*. The former Palace of The Republic being a *pars pro toto* for a complete regime, the lines allude to the contours of the former GDR without imposing any sense of monumental pretension. The decks are slightly raised and the surrounding park ground level is accessible via stairs and platforms, offering a choice between crossing through and stepping down onto the park grounds: the walker can choose which physical relationship with the controversial site he/she wishes to take. The boardwalk is but a temporary feature, yet by its strong and unequivocal atmosphere it will remain in the collective memory of Berliners for a longer time. This structure will undoubtedly develop into a welcome interlude between two topographically important periods in the long history of the square. *Die Wende* (the change in East Germany in 1989-90) will remain palpable – public and passable – in this crucial place in the city for a few years.

The design for *Kongens Have Park* is ultimately seeking a synthesis of a variety of styles (formal, picturesque and modern) which had previously been characteristic of the configuration of the site. In this sense the project is a good example of a landscape architectural abstraction of the morphological properties of the plan: the formal, 18-th century features are reflected in the axes of paths; the distribution of trees and the curved path are reminiscent of the romantic period; and the modern era is reflected in the diagonal route, the lighting features and the furniture. Thus the park has been developed as a three-dimensional collage, a topography which wants to take a little and be a little of its past history, yet has nothing specific or new to offer.

Eric Luiten is a landscape architect and planning consultant. He holds the chair of Heritage and Spatial Design at Delft University of Technology and is an independent Spatial Quality Advisor to the Provincial Board of South-Holland in The Hague. Luiten writes and talks frequently on heritage development issues, specifically from a designer's point of view. His book Design with Heritage will be published in 2012.

designed by relais Landschaftsarchitekten

SCHLOSSAREAL

Green space sloping gently to the River Spree replaces the demolished Palace of the Republic. Photos Stefan Müller

A few precise interventions in the heart of Berlin orchestrate history and give it centre stage. Where the Palace of the Republic stood until 2008, the symbol of East Germany cn the site once occupied by the palace of the kings of Prussia, is now an empty space – awaiting construction of the Humboldt Forum, which is to be the new symbol-laden architecture of unified Germany. Relais Landschaftsarchitekten laid down an expansive grassed space, sloping gently toward the River Spree, on the history-charged construction site. Wooden footbridges fashioned from rough boards subdivide and render access, while forming a solid framework. Texts and pictures here and there outline the location's chequered history. The processes of change that the expansive green space has undergone are orchestrated upon it: hitherto concealed relics of former uses – fragments of palace foundations, the boundary wall of the basement level of the Palace of the Republic – are exposed and exhibited in the style of archaeological excavations. This powerfully yet unobtrusively fashioned location – and its history with it – will remain open to the public until the Humboldt Forum is built. [cm]

Programme Temporary installation on a central remembrance site awaiting construction **Designer** relais Landschaftsarchitekten **Commissioned by** Land Berlin/ DSK **Area** 4.7 ha **Design** 2006–2008 **Implementation** 2008–2009 **Budget** € 1,400,000

Relics of former uses are displayed on the green. The palace excavations in the foreground and the stair towers of the Palace of the Republic in the background.

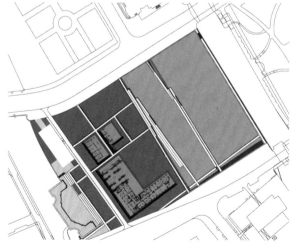

Ground plan.

BUNKER 599
designed by Rietveld Landscape | Atelier de Lyon

The stunning intervention brings a piece of recent history to life.

The massive concrete bunker was part of the military line of defence called the New Dutch Waterline (NDW). In existence from 1915 to 1940, its purpose was to protect Dutch national territory from enemy invasion by intentional inundation. Bunker 599 was preserved and is freely accessible today to visitors following the NDW trail. The artist Erick de Lyon and Rietveld Landscape agency bisected the purportedly indestructible fortification, opening up access and revealing its hitherto concealed interior. A walkway made of concrete paving stones leads right through the middle of the structure to a footbridge extending over an artificially flooded lake. The construction was preserved in remembrance of its former use; the simple but stunning intervention brings a piece of recent history to life. [cm]

Programme Landscaping of a site of remembrance **Designer** Rietveld Landscape | Atelier de Lyon **Commissioned by** DLG (The Dutch Service for Land and Water Management) **Area** 1.1 ha (Bunker 599 is 30m²) **Design** 2010 **Implementation** 2010 **Budget** € 300,000

The walkway reveals the interior and the thickness of the bunker walls.

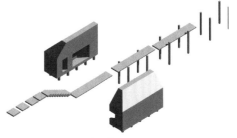

Axonometric projection.

The archaeological site at São Jorge – a landscape palimpsest. Photos Leonardo Finotti

From time immemorial, people have settled on the hill towering over Lisbon old town. Archaeological excavations in recent years have unearthed relics of the Iron Age, as well as those dating from the Middle Ages when the city was under Moorish rule, until it returned to Christian rule. Paths and steps lead today to the various excavation sites, laying bare the various chronological layers, the reading of which has been facilitated by the consistent use of materials: black basalt paths identify the contemporary layer; medieval finds lie in the areas scattered with sand of various hues, and weathering steel walls frame the Iron Age excavations that constitute the deepest layer. With great care and respect for the location, the planners have exposed its history and made it accessible to the public – a landscape palimpsest. [cm]

Programme An archaeological dig goes public **Designer** (JLCG Arquitectos and Global Arquitectura Paisagista) **Commissioned by** Municipality of Lisbon (EGEAC) **Area** 0.35 ha **Design** 2008 **Implementation** 2009–2010 **Budget** € 1,000,000

Weathering steel walls frame the excavation.

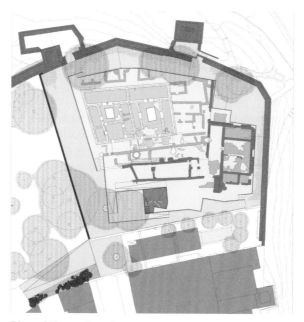

Plan of the various layers.

KONGENS HAVE PARK

designed by Erik Brandt Dam architects

The axes of the originally Baroque-styled park run contiguous to the open grassed areas of the landscape garden. Photo Helene Høyer Mikkelsen

Kongens Have Park is a typical example of a historic European park: laid out in Baroque style in 1720, the former palace grounds were redesigned in the style of a landscape garden in the 18th century and modified continually over the years. At the start of the 21st century, the park represented a heterogeneous mixture of design elements. The latest redevelopment was conceived to expose the key stylistic elements of the park's chequered history and place them in juxtaposition with one another: the axes from the Baroque period and the expansive grassed areas of the landscape garden enter into dialogue with each other today. Equally, the new design with a new lighting concept and improved accessibility meets the requirements for contemporary use as a public park. The jury appreciates the landscape architects' clarifying interventions, which have made the location's history readable while updating it at the same time. [cm]

Ground plan.

Programme Revitalization of a historic city park **Designer** Erik Brandt Dam architects **Commissioned by** Municipality of Odense **Area** 3 ha **Design** 2006–2008 **Implementation** 2009–2010 **Budget** € 1,735,000

THE URBAN FIELD

MUNICH VIENNA
ZURICH-GLATTAL

FIGUERES
VILABLAREIX

The railway line sown with low-maintenance grass is a ribbon of green running through the region. All photos Thiele & Breitschmied Fotografie

GLATTALBAHN

designed by Feddersen & Klostermann

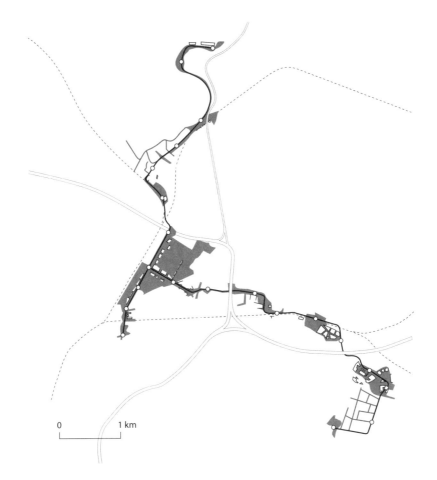

0   1 km

JURY COMMENT Infrastructure is more than an engineering task – it orients urban development strategically, and it triggers the creation of urban open space, especially in those extended and heterogeneously built-up metropolitan areas that constitute Europe's urban environments beyond the classical cities today. Glattalbahn is a strong example of an intervention that is inserted with absolute respect for the existing building stock while upgrading the area as a whole, offering it its main missing link in a high design quality. This project illustrates how urban development can be addressed as urban transformation instead of urban extension. The light rail system serves an area of the Zurich conurbation that has seen rapid development in recent decades and fragmentation as a result of a variety of infrastructural developments. The Glattal rail system is the new spine that rejoins these urban fragments and sets the pace for further development.

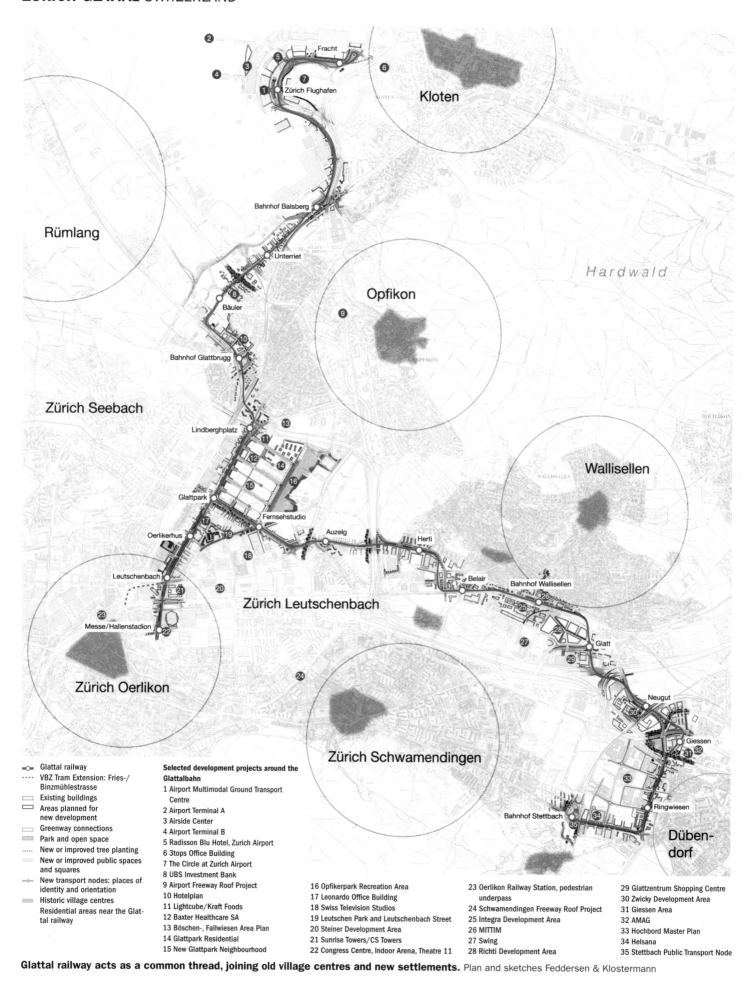

Rümlang

Kloten

Fracht

Zürich Flughafen

Bahnhof Balsberg

Unterriet

Opfikon

Bäuler

Hardwald

Bahnhof Glattbrugg

Zürich Seebach

Lindberghplatz

Wallisellen

Glattpark

Fernsehstudio

Oerlikerhus

Auzelg

Herti

Belair

Bahnhof Wallisellen

Leutschenbach

Glatt

Zürich Leutschenbach

Neugut

Messe/Hallenstadion

Giessen

Zürich Oerlikon

Zürich Schwamendingen

Ringwiesen

Bahnhof Stettbach

Düben-
dorf

Glattal railway acts as a common thread, joining old village centres and new settlements. Plan and sketches Feddersen & Klostermann

Glattal railway

VBZ Tram Extension: Fries-/
Binzmühlestrasse

Existing buildings

Areas planned for
new development

Greenway connections

Park and open space

New or improved tree planting

New or improved public spaces
and squares

New transport nodes: places of
identity and orientation

Historic village centres

Residential areas near the Glattal railway

**Selected development projects around the
Glattalbahn**

1 Airport Multimodal Ground Transport
Centre
2 Airport Terminal A
3 Airside Center
4 Airport Terminal B
5 Radisson Blu Hotel, Zurich Airport
6 3tops Office Building
7 The Circle at Zurich Airport
8 UBS Investment Bank
9 Airport Freeway Roof Project
10 Hotelplan
11 Lightcube/Kraft Foods
12 Baxter Healthcare SA
13 Böschen-, Fallwiesen Area Plan
14 Glattpark Residential
15 New Glattpark Neighbourhood

16 Opfikerpark Recreation Area
17 Leonardo Office Building
18 Swiss Television Studios
19 Leutschen Park and Leutschenbach Street
20 Steiner Development Area
21 Sunrise Towers/CS Towers
22 Congress Centre, Indoor Arena, Theatre 11

23 Oerlikon Railway Station, pedestrian
underpass
24 Schwamendingen Freeway Roof Project
25 Integra Development Area
26 MITTIM
27 Swing
28 Richti Development Area

29 Glattzentrum Shopping Centre
30 Zwicky Development Area
31 Giessen Area
32 AMAG
33 Hochbord Master Plan
34 Helsana
35 Stettbach Public Transport Node

Introducing the missing metropolitan spine

Feature by Claudia Moll

A new railway track runs through Glattal (Glatt Valley), a district to the north of Zurich, winding its way through residential, office and industrial areas as if it had always been there. The track provides a direct link between Zurich Central Station and Zurich International Airport, and a second stretch describes a wide arc connecting up the northern outskirts of Zurich. Matching, no-frills train-stops alongside the track, which is planted with low-maintenance grass, are a clear indication that the rail system did not develop in fits and starts as the area progressed; they represent a later addition conceived as a unifying concept. The hallmark of each stop is a 'Window to the City', a 7.50 x 2.40-metre glass panel that gives passers-by and waiting travellers a continuously changing glimpse of the Glattal with its heterogeneous urban landscape.

Used for farming until the 1950s, the area evolved in the second half of the 20th century to become part of a typical European conurbation. Waste incineration plants, sewage plants and a combined heat and power station grew up around small villages. A dense network of infrastructure including train platforms, freeways and their feeders came to lie on the banks of the Glatt, the stream that gives the valley its name. Fields dotted here and there and the old-style cores of former villages are relics of the valley's former role, and nature reserves alongside the river indicate its origins as a swampy habitat – but the former farming villages have long since merged and become part of the conurbation. At the joins, densely utilized residential, office and service centres arose with no clear structures or mutual links.

Nonetheless, the area does not correspond with the cliché of a bleak periphery. It has developed during the last two decades from being the back end of Zurich into a new urban centre of importance for the whole of Switzerland. Thanks to its ready accessibility – from the heavily expanding Zurich International Airport and the metropolis of Zurich – a host of national and transnational companies have set up business here. The valley is Switzerland's largest development area today. Office, industrial and residential buildings are springing up in many new city districts. An example is Glattpark, zoned to provide 7000 jobs and living space for 7000 new residents in two stages. The faceless suburban area has in that way evolved in recent years to a 'pretty perfect periphery' – as it was called by the architect Mario Campi in his book published in 2001 *(Annähernd perfekte Peripherie, Glattalstadt)*. The eight municipalities it incorporates now see themselves as a Netzstadt (networked city). If they were to team up as a single city, it would be Switzerland's fourth largest with a population of 150,000.

All the people who live and work here need mobility. However, the existing infrastructures, in particular the road network, have not kept pace with the breakneck speed of development and rapidly reached the limits of their capacity. This situation was predicted more than 20 years ago by the heads of four of the municipalities concerned. They initiated the setting up of the Glattal Future Lobby (Interessengemeinschaft Zukunft Glattal, IG Zug) in 1990 with the aim of establishing a joint light rail system. It was to be a high-tech public transport resource, something between an *S-Bahn* city train and local bus, that would link the main centres of population with each other and encourage people to abandon car travel in favour of public transport. IG Zug's ideas were largely compatible with the overarching population and transport policy goals of the governing council of the canton of Zurich. As a result, this ambitious project spanning multiple municipalities was able to advance at a swift pace. It was included in the cantonal town planning books in 1995; in 1998, Glattal Transport Association (VBG Verkehrsbetriebe Glattal AG) was appointed to plan the new transport system. The electorate of the canton of Zurich approved funding in 2003, and the three stages in the rail system were handed over to the public at two-year intervals starting from 2006.

It now constitutes the common thread joining the disparate parts of Glattal valley. The route it follows runs through the peripheries, not the centres of the original municipalities, in that way helping to turn the heterogeneous 'in-between' into an integral part of the new *Netzstadt*. Two key factors make the transport system an identity-building structure for the entire area. Firstly, the planners rejected early on the notion of a rail system that would be just one more axis bisecting urban space (e.g. a space-saving overhead railway or high-speed magnetic railway). Instead, they wanted a new light rail system that would be an integral part of the public space, which means it had to be level with the city as such. It was not always an easy decision to carry through given the confined spaces available, but definitely the right one for the city as an organism. It also implied that the planning perimeter would not end at the edge of the line but would have to extend from facade to facade. The fact that the transport system is perceived as a coherent entity is also due to the uniform design of the train stops. The three-dimensional wall panel with the Window to the City protects waiting travellers from wind and the overhanging roof provides shelter from the rain. A ticket machine, timetables, loudspeaker and waste container are integrated in the modular wall panel. The larchwood frame surrounding the Window to the City doubles as a large bench to sit on. The railings attached to the stops, bicycle stands and contact line systems are also of uniform design. The recurrent elements contribute to the Glattalbahn being perceived as a unit and help it to fit into its heterogeneous environment.

The project, consistently thought through at every level, is the brainchild of a large team composed of environmental planners, town planners, architects and landscape architects, environment and transport planners, civil engineers and railway engineers. All of them looked upon the task as a cooperative planning process in which everyone concerned had to think and act beyond the limits of their own discipline. The best solutions for all parties were continuously sought in an intensive process of dialogue involving 80 agencies, and property owners and locals were included in the discussions. That effort is paying off today. The rail met with a high level of public acceptance from the start and has been a veritable catalyst of development for the region. The latest studies put the total expected private investment along the railway line for the 2001-2005 period at more than € 7.5 billion – about 16 times as much as it cost to build the rail system.

As befits projects of these dimensions, a monument to mark the achievement was mooted upon completion. One politician proposed an attractive natural stone fountain with a plaque engraved with the main names and dates. Again, the team members managed to agree upon a solution, al-

beit unconventional: instead of building a fountain, they columnar oak trees. Sets of six trees planted in a circle in 10 places by the track are set to grow into landmarks as the years go by. They stand for the six municipalities involved in the construction project and for the six quality goals the project set out to meet: social compatibility, environmental compatibility, cost-effectiveness on the one hand, coupled with fitness for purpose, safety and durability on the other.

Programme Light rail connecting six municipalities in the northern metropolitan area of Zurich **Designer** Feddersen & Klostermann (Rainer Klostermann, Kai Flender, Philipp Rüegg, André Seippel) **In collaboration with** Planning and project design were done in interdisciplinary teams involving more than 80 agencies for town and country planning, urban development, architecture, environment, civil engineering, transport, railway construction and railway engineering. Approximately 70 companies were involved in performing the work. **Commissioned by** VBG Verkehrs-betriebe Glattal AG, on behalf of Zurich Canton and the Swiss Confederation (conurbation policy) **Area** 12.7 km new stretch of track **Design** 1998–2004 **Implementation** 2004–2010, start-up in three stages (2006, 2008, 2010). **Budget** Total investment €460,000,000 approx. (core project)

in stops of uniform design in front of new commercial buildings on the outskirts of the city.

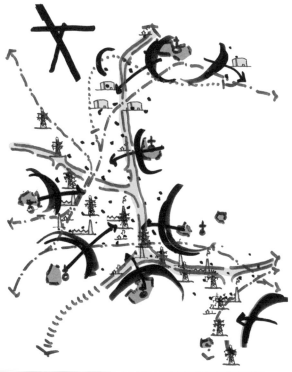
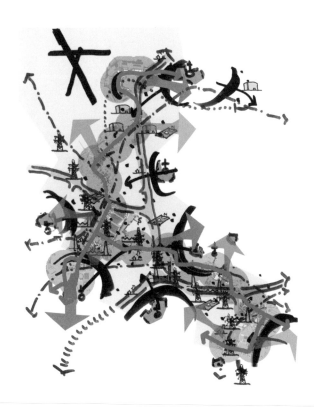

evelopment of the Glattal area: breaking out – filling in – networking.

On the way to the airport, Glattalbahn runs through the last fields in the region still used for agriculture.

The new light rail winds its way through the dense periphery.

...cles of trees will grow into landmarks in decades to come.

A flowering carpet covers the railway line in summertime.
Photo Feddersen & Klostermann

The uniform design applies to the railings too.

The frame surrounding the Window to the City doubles as a place to sit and wait.

Essay by Svava Riesto, Martin Søberg and Ellen Braae

CITY OF OPEN WORKS

Cities change – and so do the tasks and agendas of landscape architects. New types of urban schemes are increasingly arising. On the one hand, new sorts of commissions have emerged in recent years – on the other hand, traditional commissions have been interpreted in radically new ways. These contemporary approaches are closely connected to challenges following the transformation of existing urban structures – the re-use of metropolis. And the resulting projects are often created as more or less open works; they challenge existing typologies through a particularly inclusive and heterogeneous design method. But what actually characterizes this new design method? We have identified five specific strategies, described below.

BEGIN WITH THE PRE-EXISTENT. Well-defined and familiar urban typologies such as the park, the square and the perimeter block courtyard are hard to find in many contemporary projects. Rather, we frequently witness hybrids of existing types and new modes of urban public space as most of the sites were already urbanized before the design intervention: for landscape architects tabula rasa situations are non-existent. But as the projects we refer to may prove, many landscape architects consider both tangible and intangible layers of a site as generative for design: not as a restraint to universal ideas, but as a stepping stone towards creative attitudes and complex public open spaces. Manuel Ruisánchez' *Güell River Park* in Vilablareix and Realgrün's *Hirschgarten and Pionierpark* in Munich, exemplify this approach by their ability to reinvent public open space in urbanized areas: the heterogeneity of an existing urban area is retained and strengthened, resulting in varied public spaces with multiple different atmospheres and possibilities for a broad range of uses and users.

The sites to work on have changed. Contemporary reinventions of urban public space are closely related to the nature of the sites that landscape architects are commissioned to handle. The de-industrialization of many European cities has taken place for many decades and accelerated within the past 10 to 15 years, a development that has cast off abandoned production plants, massive distribution areas, and other large industrial structures in the urbanized parts of Europe. Most of the icons in this section of the book are situated on railway tracks or other significant infrastructural complexes built in the 19th and 20th centuries. Decisions to redevelop such industrial complexes into other urban functions indicate socio-economic changes. This is also connected to a renewed attraction of metropolitan lifestyles with roots going back to the late 1970s, when young, poor artists began to reclaim abandoned production buildings – such as those found in Berlin's Kreuzberg area or the New York lofts. Living, working and using the city centre made it an attractive alternative to the suburbs. More recently, environmental concerns are a prime reason for reusing existing structures rather than relying on demolition.

PUBLIC SPACES ARE OPEN GAMES. Redeveloping existing, often industrial urban structures has become an arena for rethinking the city as such. While many urban sites are characterized by modern planning's segregation into industrial-, housing-, or infrastructural functions, recent projects show an urge to combine multiple uses. Contemporary interventions frequently strive to strengthen the relationship between the commissioned site and other agents within the urban tissue. As programmes and uses of the city change, so do our ideas of what a city is and should be. This prompts us to question which roles the public sphere plays in the contemporary city and which role it should play in the future. And not least: which role should designers play in the development of urban public spaces? In their new neighbourhood *Les Horts de Vilabertran* in Figueres, Michele & Miquel have chosen a subtle role. The park is a complex mesh of open and intimate spaces that offer an open chequer board of programmes. This space can be appropriated by multiple activities and users, which are not predetermined by the commissioner or the landscape architects. New modes of public interaction have emerged. Alternative ways of using urban spaces have developed, in mutual exchange with new spatial types and physical characteristics. This renaissance of public urban life is, nevertheless, often characterized by focusing on individual activities, on groups of people with common interests, who share certain agendas and which might even exclude others.

EPITOMIZE MOTION. Yet leave room for complexity: many recent projects appear to be based on an understanding of the city as consisting of various layers through a design that exposes temporal and spatial synchronicity. Different historical layers inform each other and interrelate in the new design, as do other aspects of the site with both global and local relevance. Also, the flow of the city is often alluded to. Many projects comprise an idea or materialization of motion. Flow is recognized in existing lines of infrastructure on site and is also introduced in innovative ways with new pathways, roads and bike lanes. The sense of being in transition is strengthened by the use of ruderal plants as shown in *Hirschgarten and Pionierpark* in Munich. Furthermore, these projects cling to images of flow in their formal organization; parallel stripes, fragmented rows of trees and barcodes.

Schweingruber Zulauf Landschaftsarchitekten's foot- and cycle path on the former *Lettenviadukt* in Zurich is an example of the tendency of temporal/spatial montage that emphasizes various modes of movement and layers of the city. The transformation of the former railway viaduct into a transportation route for pedestrians and cyclists has changed the perception of the surroundings in so far as people are now able to move at a considerably different height than when the viaduct was restricted to trains. One experiences the extreme speeds of the trains beneath when walking along the upper part of the viaduct – a large amount of trains from Zurich Airport to Zurich Central Station are among the ones on this route – while locals sip coffee in cosy cafés under the arches of the viaduct. Various urban and temporal scales are linked in this way: a global network that allows fast moves, while the rough materiality of the viaduct's stones and new concrete paving – the latter alluding to the visual expression of railway tracks – ensure a material, sensorial presence. Rather than being separated, different functions, scales and atmospheres are layered and interact.

DESIGN WITH TIME. Temporal aspects have always been part of landscape architecture. But today, even the design of many other projects is temporal and open. The latter correlates with what might be termed soft programming, which implies including a broad range of possible future uses, which are not necessarily specified in advance. Hager Partner's *Rudolf-Bednar-Park* in Vienna is at first sight a rather traditional urban park, spatially defined by the surrounding blocks. But it is organized according to a striped structure that differentiates flows; moving from an active part on the south-western side of the park to the more quiet, residential part on the north-east. This structure enables users to cross diagonally from one temporal sphere to another.

Today, many landscape architects are engaging directly with history. However, there are multiple answers as to why landscape architectural projects should tell stories about the past. Why mimic the railway line once here at all? What should projects communicate? The ability of places touched by landscape architects to allow for new interpretations by users and let them be associated with new stories, determines the degree of openness of a work. Openness concerns how the project is inscribed in the city, its functions as well as its room for interpretation. What already exists on site can be used as a conceptual starting point. This seems to be the approach behind the *Güell River Park*, for which the river that was once there is a structuring element. While elements from the past can structure the overall disposition of a new project, other approaches are also possible. Another part of the spectrum is to use aspects of the site as a narrative or image that depicts previous forms and uses. Such approaches pose questions about the power of interpretation – who makes these stories, on behalf of whom, and for whom? To what extent is the project interpretable according to some pre-defined intentions of a privileged author? How open is the project for alternative readings and uses of the sites – by weaker groups and by future users as yet unknown?

INTERVENE RATHER THAN INVENT. An attitude of openness often characterizes those projects where landscape architects consider their job to be an intervention rather than invention: projects that emphasize that their task is to transform an existing urban situation and to appropriate certain existing conditions rather than inventing something completely new. By creating open works rather than striving to become an omniscient master who creates fixed works of art, the landscape architect opens up a dialogue. This requires attention to what is already there at the site and implies preserving selected elements or structures open for both current and future interventions and interpretations. Such an approach, stressing the unfinished, the non-stable, embraces and assimilates existing, and often very heterogeneous elements. A tension between keeping a loose structure of an open field of elements and introducing diversity within a new coherent visual expression characterizes these projects, made by landscape architects who are willing to embrace existing conditions and physical structures, spatial and material differences, in order to create rich and interesting new urban public spaces as open works within a larger, urban context.

Svava Riesto, PhD, is an art historian doing post-doctoral work in the Research Group for Landscape architecture and -urbanism, University of Copenhagen, where she also teaches Theory and Method of Landscape Architecture.

Martin Søberg is an art historian conducting PhD research at the Royal Danish Academy of Fine Arts, Schools of Architecture, Design and Conservation, Institute of Building Culture. His thesis is on architectural drawing and artistic research.

Ellen Braae, PhD, is professor and head of the Research Group for Landscape architecture and -urbanism as well as head of studies for MSc

LES HORTS DE VILABERTRAN

designed by Michele & Miquel architects & landscape designers

The original atmosphere lives on this green backbone of a new district.

The growth of a new residential area is planned in the immediate vicinity of the centre of the small town of Figueres on former farmland. Exposed to wind and sun, the irrigated plot was clearly structured: natural stone walls, a system of water-courses, irrigation channels and retention basins, fruit trees and wind-breaking cypresses were its main features. The landscape architects proposed preserving major parts of the existing landscape to create a park 'as found' rather than construct-ing a new one, while inserting the residential areas in a meaningful manner. They added new landscape elements required for urban use to the existing landscape and wove the various chrono-logical layers into a new whole. A weathering steel footbridge leads across the former fields, a long bench flanks the row of cypresses, and new chan-nels have been added to take some of the water that flows through the park. The original atmos-phere of the place lives on in the green backbone of the new district, with the addition of an indi-vidual, culturally founded quality. [cm]

A footbridge leads across the former fields.

Programme Masterplan for residential area on former farm-land including park **Designer** Michele & Miquel architects & landscape designers (Michèle Orliac, Miquel Batlle) **In collaboration with** Dimitry Khomyakov, Eleanora Barone (assistant architects) Miquel Àngel Sala BOMA (Structure) Jordi Quera, Esteve Riba; Enigest S.L. (urbanization and installation) Juanjo Martínez (vegetation) Guillem Lacoma (irrigation) **Commissioned by** Institut Català del Sòl **Area** 14.5 ha **Design** 2006 **Implementation** 2007–2009 **Budget** € 9,220,500

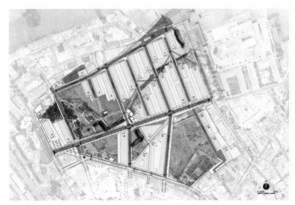

Ground plan.

The elongated Pionierpark mediates between railway area and new buildings. Photo Klaus-D. Neumann

A new residential and business district has been developed over the past number of years to replace the former container terminal on the stretch of track in front of Munich Central Station. According to urban development plans, the disused section of track alongside the platforms was to be the site of an elongated park connecting the new buildings with the railway areas. A continuous cycle and pedestrian path was to link western suburban districts with the city centre. The landscape architects retained the characteristic ruderal vegetation of the former container terminal, accentuating the contrast with the carefully designed environment of the new buildings behind. They extended the existing Hirschgarten landscape park with a meadow with trees, added a strip of land equipped with a sports and skatepark, and continued it into the Pionierpark. The landscape architects developed the various open spaces from materials already in place. The outcome is a mosaic of open spaces of various designs that are suitable for a range of uses. [cm]

Sports fields and a skatepark are located between Pionierpark and the new grassy area planted with trees. Photo Kai Gettner

Programme Redevelopment of a former railway area and extension of an existing park **Designer** realgrün Landschaftsarchitekten (Wolf D. Auch, Klaus-D. Neumann) **In collaboration with** Erwin Rechsteiner (skatepark consultant) Christoph Ackermann (stress analyst) **Commissioned by** Aurelis Real Estate GmbH&Co.KG (park areas) and City of Munich, Department of Public Construction (skatebowl) **Area** 6.2 ha **Design** 2007 **Implementation** 2007–2010 **Budget** € 6,460,000

RUDOLF-BEDNAR-PARK

designed by Hager Partner AG

The reed gardens are a reminiscent of the river Danube, which had a deep impact on the formation of the area in the past. Photo Rupert Steiner

The park is the main element of the public space for a new residential and working area that is emerging on the land of the disused former freight rail terminal in Vienna's second district. A rectangular area carved from the development zone, the park was laid out before the buildings and is becoming a driver of social interaction in this culturally heterogeneous part of the city. The distinguishing features are the lines of trees. In total there are about 280 trees, in which about five different species are represented. They trace the direction of the former rail tracks and the River Danube, which flows nearby. At the edges of the park, hedges and flower beds structure the site and set out areas suitable for a variety of uses: places to retreat as well as playing areas. The lines of trees end toward the middle, and the centre of the park is an open green space. Although the rigorous conformation may to some of the jury members not be entirely convincing, the 'Green before Urban' approach certainly is. [cm]

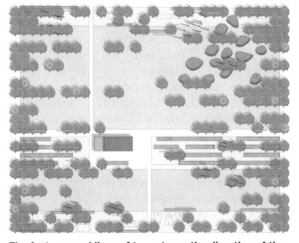

The features and lines of trees trace the direction of the former rail tracks and the River Danube.

Programme Urban park **Designer** Hager Partner AG **Commissioned by** Municipal Department of Parks and Gardens, City of Vienna, MA 42 **Area** 4 ha **Design** 2006–2007 **Implementation** 2007–2008 **Budget** € 5,550,000

In the event of flooding, the park acts as an ecological compensation area. Photo Shlomi Almagor

The small town of Vilablareix in Catalonia has expanded southward in recent years. New urban structures have grown up where hedgerows formerly divided the plain into separate fields. Güell River Park is the green backbone of a planned residential area and separates it from the adjoining industrial estate. It integrates the bed and the thick riparian vegetation of the diverted Güell River, a typical Mediterranean dry river that is a dry depression for most of the year and only carries water during seasonal downpours, but then in abundance. Arranged in terraces and situated two metres lower than the adjacent road, the park acts as a flood plain when water levels rise. The designers incorporated traditional types of vegetation as structuring elements: the dense belt of hedges that used to accompany the river is now an extensive park boundary, and the trees planted in grids are reminiscent of the compact clusters of trees that studded the formerly agricultural plain. Ramps, embankments and broad paths made from concrete slabs cast on site connect the terraced levels, which are suitable for a variety of uses; two wooden bridges lead to the new part of the town. It is impressive to see how this common space both meets hydraulic needs and serves the public: as a riverbed and as a park. [cm]

Programme Strip of park with drainage for a new urban district **Designer** Manuel Ruisánchez Architect (Anna Bonet, Ana Elisa Neto, Vincent Parasie, Anna Casals, Felipe Peña) **In collaboration with** Manel Colominas (agronomic engineer) **Commissioned by** Junta de Compensació de Pla Parcial El Perelló i Can Pere Màrtir **Area** 3.5 ha **Design** 2006 **Implementation** 2008–2009 **Budget** € 3,513,000

designed by Manuel Ruisánchez Architect

GÜELL RIVER PARK

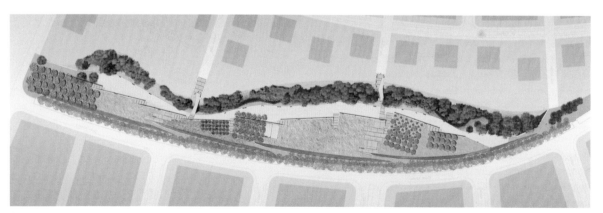

Ground plan.

LETTENVIADUKT

designed by Schweingruber Zulauf Landschaftsarchitekten

The pedestrian and cycle path, five metres above street level, opens up new perspectives on the urban fabric.
Photos René Rötheli

The former industrial area in the western part of Zurich has been in transition for some years. The railway viaduct overhead – the Lettenviadukt – carried trains until the 1990s and fell into disuse for more than a decade before its new purpose was decided upon. It now acts as a pedestrian and cycle path that connects the recently extended public spaces on Limmat with the ever more popular city district. In a parallel development, a market hall and shops moved into the adjacent arches of the higher Wipkinger Viadukt, which still carries trains. The design of the route is plain but convincing: in their simplicity and rhythmic repetition, the concrete paving stones, seating elements and masts line up and mimic the language of railway architecture. Gravel strips beside the paths emphasize this reference and serve as a habitat for the lizards that came to inhabit the disused line. The location five metres above street level opens up new diverse perspectives on the urban fabric, and the re-used viaduct retraces the district's social transition. [cm]

Programme Redesign of a former railway viaduct **Designer** Schweingruber Zulauf Landschaftsarchitekten **In collaboration with** EM2N Architekten (viaduct arches) **Commissioned by** Civil Engineering Department of the City of Zurich (main commissioner), Swiss Rail, PWG Foundation **Area** 0.283 ha **Design** 2004 **Implementation** 2008–2010 **Budget** € 3,600,000

The path connects the open spaces in the district and is very well used.

Seating elements.

1 ANTWERP
SCHELDT QUAYS [PROAP, OS]
2 L'AMPOLLA
CAP ROIG RESIDENTIAL DEVELOP-
MENT [Michèle & Miquel, F]
3 AMSTERDAM
DE NIEUWE OOSTER CEMETERY
[Karres en Brands, F]
ENCLOSED GARDEN [Anouk
Vogel, IT]
FUNENPARK [LANDLAB, IT]
THE OLYMPIC STADIUM'S URBAN
FIELD [Buro Sant en Co, OS]
VONDELPARK CANOPY WALK
[Carve, IT]
4 ARNHEM
MONNIKENHUIZEN SETTLEMENT
[Buro Lubbers, F]
5 ATHENS
HELLENIKON METROPOLITAN
PARK [Iterae Architecture, Office
of Landscape Morphology, F]
6 BADALUCCO
MATTEOTTI SQUARE [mag.MA
architetture, IT]
7 BAD ESSEN
GARDEN OF BABEL [Klahn +
Singer + Partner, F]
8 BARAKALDO
PLAZA DEL DESIERTO [NOMAD
Arquitectos S.L., F]
9 BARCELONA
MIMOSA COURTYARD [Bet
Figueras, IT]
10 BEGUR
PRIVATE GARDEN [Bet Figueras,
IT]
11 BENAVENTE
PARQUE RIBEIRINHO [NPK, OS]
12 BERLIN
MASELAKEPARK [relais
Landschaftsarchitekten, OS]
OPEN SPACES IN SPREEBOGEN
[Lützow 7, F]
SCHLOSSAREAL [relais Land-
schaftsarchitekten, F]
TILLA DURIEUX PUBLIC PARK [DS
Landschapsarchitecten, F]
TOPOGRAPHY OF TERROR [Martin
Prominski, Imke Woelk und Partner,
OS]
13 BERN
HARDEGG RESIDENTIAL AREA
[Rotzler Krebs, IT]
14 BEVEREN
RECREATED NATURE [OSA –
Katholieke Universiteit Leuven, OS]
15 BILBAO
MASTERPLAN ZORROTZAURRE
[GROSS.MAX., OS]
URBAN GARDEN [Anouk Vogel,
IT]
16 BORDEAUX
JARDIN BOTANIQUE [Mosbach
Paysagistes, F]
MIROIR D'EAU [Michel Corajoud,
Pierre Gangnet, Jean-Max Llorca,
OS]
OPEN SPACES FOR TRAM [Bro-
chet-Lajus-Pueyo, Groupe Signes,
Elisabeth de Portzamparc, OS]
17 BUTTIKON
GROUNDS FOR OBERMARCH
SCHOOL [Stefan Koepfli, F]
18 CADAQUÉS
CAP DE CREUS [Estudi Martí
Franch and Ardevols Associats,
IT]

19 COIMBRA
GARDEN OF THE CERCA DE SAO
BERNARDO [Margem, F]
MONDEGO GREEN PARK'S WEST-
ERN ENTRANCE [PROAP, OS]
20 COPENHAGEN
BERTEL THORVALDSENS PLADS
[Schønherr, F]
COURTYARD IN CLASSENGADE
[1:1 Landskab, IT]
PRAGS BOULEVARD [Kristine
Jensens Tegnestue, F]
THE CITY DUNE [SLA, IT]
21 CULEMBORG
BUNKER 599 [Rietveld Land-
scape/Atelier de Lyon, IT]
22 DESSAU
THE IBA STADTUMBAU [Station
C23, OS]
23 DRENTHE
DRENTSCHE AA LANDSCAPE
[Strootman, OS]
STRUBBEN KNIPHORSTBOSCH
[Strootman, IT]
24 DUBLIN
FATHER COLLINS PARK [Abelleyro
+ Romero Architects, F]
25 EINDHOVEN
WATERRIJK DISTRICT [Juurlink +
Geluk, Architectuurstudio HH, OS]
26 ELVAS
ROSSIO DE SÃO FRANCISCO
[LoDo arquitectura paisagista, OS]
27 ENSCHEDE
VAN HEEKPLEIN MARKET SQUARE
[OKRA, F]
28 ESPLUGUES DE LLOBREGAT
TORRENT D'EN FARRÉ PUBLIC
PARK [Isabel Bennasar Félix, F]
29 ESSEN
MECHTENBERG FIELDS [Studio
Bürgi, F]
ZOLLVEREIN PARK [Agence Ter,
Planergruppe Oberhausen, OS]
30 ÉVORA
ÉVORA'S MUNICIPAL GROVE [Luís
Alçada Baptista, OS]
31 FIGUERES
LES HORTS DE VILABERTRAN
[Michele&Miquel, F]
32 FINALE LIGURIA
ISASCO GARDEN ESTATE [CZstudio
architettura paesaggio, OS]
33 FREDERIKSBERG
FREDERIKSBERG'S CITY CENTRE
[SLA, OS]
34 FRIESLAND
WADDEN COAST LANDSCAPE
VISION [Buro Harro, IT]
35 GLASGOW
ROTTENROW GARDENS [GROSS.
MAX, F]
36 GRONINGEN
FARMYARDS IN HOGELAND
[Veenenbos en Bosch, F]
37 HAGENDORN
GROUNDS OF THE WINDOW
FACTORY [Koepfli Landschafts-
architekten, Graber und Steiger
Architekten, OS]
38 HANOVER
COURTYARD OF THE OLD
HAHN PRINTING PRESS [relais
Landschaftsarchitekten, OS]
39 HERNING
HEART'S OPEN SPACES [Schøn-
herr, F]

40 HOLLAND AND UTRECHT
HOLLAND'S GREEN HEART
[H+N+S, F]
41 IVRY-SUR-SEINE
PARC DES CORMAILLES [Agence
Ter, OS]
42 JÜCHEN
CARGO GARDEN [relais
Landschaftsarchitekten, F]
THE NEW GARDENS IN
THE DYCK FIELD [RMP
Landschaftsarchitekten, F]
43 KOCEVJE
GROUNDS FOR OB RINZI SCHOOL
[Ana Kučan, F]
44 LAUSANNE
GARDEN ON CASTLE SQUARE
[Anouk Vogel, IT]
45 LA VALL D'EN JOAN
LANDFILL LANDSCAPE [Battle i
Roig Arquitectes, F]
46 LE HAVRE
JARDIN PORTUAIRE [Thilo Folkerts
Landschaftsarchitektur, F]
47 LEIPZIG
GRÜNER BOGEN PAUNSDORF
[Häfner/Jiménez Landschafts-
architekten, OS]
48 LES PRESES
PEDRA TOSCA PARK [RCR Arqui-
tectes, OS]
49 LISBON
SAO JORGE CASTLE [JLCG Arqui-
tectos and Global Arquitectura
Paisagista, IT]
TAGUS CYCLE TRACK [Global
Arquitectura Paisagista and
PO6, IT]
50 LOCARNO
CARDADA GEOLOGICAL OBSER-
VATORY AND TRAILS [Paolo L.
Bürgi, F]
**51 LOFOTEN AND HELGELAND
COAST**
VIEWPOINTS ALONG THE TOUR-
IST ROUTE [Inge Dahlmann
LANDSKAPSFABRIKKEN, OS]
52 LONDON
NORMAND PARK [Kinnear, IT]
PLAYGROUNDS FOR DAUBENEY
PRIMARY SCHOOL [Kinnear, F]
POTTERS FIELDS PARK [GROSS.
MAX., OS]
53 LJUBLJANA
TIVOLI UNDERPASS [prostoRoz, IT]
54 MAGDEBURG
OPEN AIR LIBRARY [Karo*, IT]
55 MANCHESTER
ANCOATS PUBLIC REALM [Camlin
Lonsdale, OS]
56 MARGHERA
CATENE PARK [CZstudio associati,
IT]
57 MECHELEN
MELAAN STREETSCAPE [OKRA,
OS]
58 MUNICH
ALLIANZ ARENA [Vogt, OS]
FÜNF HÖFE COURTYARDS AND
ROOFTOPS [Burger Landschafts-
architekten, OS]
HIRSCHGARTEN AND PIONIER-
PARK [realgrün, IT]
ISAR RIVER BANKS [Irene Burk-
hardt Landschaftsarchitekten, F]
LANDSCHAFTSPARK RIEM
[Latitude Nord, F]

PLAYSCAPES AT RIEM PARK
[Rainer Schmidt, Burger Land-
schaftsarchitekten, OS]
PLATZ DER MENSCHENRECHTE
[Valentien + Valentien, OS]
59 NAPLES
AMBITO 13 [Studio Gasparrini,
OS]
60 NØRRESUNDBY
NØRRESUNDBY HARBOUR'S
URBAN GARDEN [SLA, OS]
61 ODDA
MARKETPLACE AND WATERFRONT
[Bjørbekk & Lindheim, F]
62 ODENSE
KONGENS HAVE PARK [Erik
Brandt Dam, IT]
63 PADULA
PINECONE GARDEN [West 8, OS]
64 PARIS
JARDIN SAUVAGE [atelier le
balto, F]
LES JARDINS D'ÉOLE [Michel et
Claire Corajoud, ADR Architectes,
Georges Descombes, OS]
65 POTSDAM
WALDPARK POTSDAM [B+B, F]
66 PRAGUE
TERRACES OF THE NOVY SMÍCHOV
SHOPPING CENTRE [D3A spol.
s.r.o., F]
67 RAPPERSWIL
CITYHAUS PLAZA [Blau und Gelb,
OS]
68 REYKJAVIK
MUSEUM COURTYARD INSTALLA-
TION [Martha Schwartz, IT]
69 ROME
FORUM ROMANUM WALKWAY
[Nemesi Studio, F]
URBAN PARK IN CASAL MONAS-
TERO [Osa architettura e paesag-
gio, OS]
70 ROTTERDAM
AFRIKAANDERPLEIN [OKRA, OS]
NIEUW-TERBREGGE OBSERVA-
TORIUM [Observatorium, F]
71 SALOU
SALOU SEAFRONT PROMENADE
[Jordi Bellmunt, Xavier Andreu, F]
72 SANKT GALLEN
CITY LOUNGE IN THE RAIFFEISEN
QUARTER [Pipilotti Rist, Carlos
Martinez Architects, OS]
73 SELJORD
SELJORD LAKE SITES [Rintala
Eggertson/Feste/Springer, IT]
74 SERMANGE
HEART OF THE VILLAGE [Agence
Territoires, IT]
75 SIDENSJÖ
TWO PIERS [GORA art&landscape,
OS]
76 SIERRE
JARDINS DE L'HÔTEL DE VILLE ET
DE LA POSTE [4d AG Landschafts-
architekten, OS]
77 SILEA
CENDON DI SILEA RIVERSIDE
[made associati, F]
78 SOLOTHURN
ST NIKLAUS GARDEN OF RE-
MEMBRANCE [w+s Landschafts-
architekten, F]
79 TREFFORT-CUISIAT
CHAMP DE FOIRE [Michèle &
Miquel, OS]

80 TULLAMORE
SCULPTURE PARK BOORA BO
[Dermot Foley, IT]
81 TWENTE
HUB FARMS [van Paridon X d
Groot, IT]
82 UMEÅ
NORRLANDS HOSPITAL GARD
[GORA art & landscape, F]
83 UNTERFÖHRING
GROUNDS IN THE PARK VILLA
OFFICE COMPLEX [Burger
Landschaftsarchitekten, F]
84 UTRECHT
ACOUSTIC BARRIER AT LEIDS
RIJN [ONL, F]
85 VAUD COUNTY
THE CADRAGES LANDSCAPE
STUDY [Verzone Woods Archite
OS]
86 VENETO COUNTY
GREEN BYPASS [MetroPlan
Architettura Ingegneria, OS]
87 VIENNA
RUDOLF-BEDNAR-PARK [Hage
Partner AG, IT]
88 VILABLAREIX
GÜELL RIVER PARK [Manuel
Ruisánchez Architect, IT]
89 WABERN
SWISSTOPO [Katja Schenker, (
90 WEIACH
STADLERSTRASSE [vl.
vo.architecture.landscape, IT]
WEIACH CHURCHYARD [Kuhn
Truninger, F]
91 WEINGARTEN
WEINGARTEN CITY GARDEN
[Lohrer.Hochrein Landschafts-
architekten BDLA, F]
92 WIERINGEN
WIERINGEN PASSAGE [Strootn
Palmboom & van den Bout, OS
93 WINTERTHUR
BRÜHLGUTPARK [Rotzler Krebs
IT]
94 ZURICH
GLATTALBAHN [Feddersen &
Klostermann, IT]
HOUSING LEIMBACHSTRASSE
[Berchtold.Lenzin, pool Archite
ten, OS]
KATZENBACH CENTRAL SQUAR
[Robin Winogrond Landschaft
architekten, IT]
LETTENAREAL [Rotzler Krebs, O
LETTENVIADUKT [Schweingrub
Zulauf, IT]

This map shows the selected p
jects for Landscape Architectur
Europe of In Touch (IT) and the
previous editions On Site (200
OS) and Fieldwork (2006, F).

Cap de Creus project in Cadaqués.
Previous pages: Visiting Rome during the presentation of the first LAE book *Fieldwork*.

Sixty years - Finding a common approach to context, history, natural strata

Essay by Meto Vroom

The Landscape Architecture Europe Foundation (LAE) came into being in 2002, when I witnessed the passing of the Deed of Incorporation at the office of a notary public in Wageningen. Ten years later the Foundation has published *In Touch*, the third book in a series of triennial overviews of current best practice in Europe. Since 2002, eight years after my retirement in 1994 as professor of landscape architecture in Wageningen, I have served as chairman of the Board of the Foundation. Now that the moment has arrived to hand over the chairmanship to the present jury chairman, Michael van Gessel, it seems appropriate to reflect on (some of the) developments and changes over a period of more than sixty years during which I have been involved in the landscape architecture profession, and also on some of the dilemmas the LAE Foundation faces.

A WAY OUT OF A DILEMMA. A major dilemma is the need to present as many selected projects as possible within a book of normal size and at an affordable price. The LAE books are aimed at a wide audience of professionals. This calls for a succinct and very accessible overview of every project. The reader wants to know the answer to such questions as: What is this and where? How does it relate to its environment? How is it composed and how does it function? Why is it pronounced as being of high quality? How did they do this? And what is where? The only way to show the selected projects in a book is by means of photographs, plans and perspectives accompanied by explanatory text; and this severely limits the amount of information conveyed, even if one may assume that the readers (or at least most of them) have been trained in the interpretation of graphic representations. They are expected to be able to 'look through' a drawing.

As the French philosopher Bruno Latour states, '...four hundred years after the invention of perspective drawing, three hundred years after projective geometry, fifty years after the development of computer screens, we are still utterly unable to draw together, to simulate, to materialize, to approximate, to fully model to scale, what a thing in all of its complexity is.' The dilemma is therefore how to present selected projects in a condensed way and yet provide a maximum of information with the means available. *In Touch* tackles this problem by dividing the selected entries in two categories, one of which is analyzed more in depth. This is a first step towards placing more emphasis on the role of research in design.

CHANGES OVER TIME. When reviewing the major changes in outlook, values and design styles over a period of sixty years and comparing these with recent projects presented in the three LAE books published so far, I see a great deal of change and diversity among the individual schemes. But I also recognize continuity and constancy. Many of the formerly held ideals may have been discarded – rejected for a while – but eventually they tend to reappear again in various forms. In the meantime the scope of assignments over the years has expanded in a remarkable way.

LESSONS OF MODERNISM – THE 1950S. During the 1950s I was a student of landscape architecture, first at Wageningen University (under Professor Jan Bijhouwer) and later, for two years at the School of Fine Arts of the University of Pennsylvania (under Professor Ian McHarg). At the time I was confronted with the ideals of modernism prevailing in Europe as well as the USA. In the following decades, when I became a practitioner and later a teacher, I witnessed some profound changes in ideas and ideals in landscape architecture, even though some of the early dreams remained valid. In the early fifties modernism was a relatively new phenomenon for landscape architects and for a beginning student the exposure to its ideals was a novel and exciting experience. Modernism was associated with a political ideology, a dogma and a design style. The dogmas have since been abandoned but the dominant aesthetic principles are still recognizable in contemporary designs.

The new credo of the modernist was that forms, colours, textures and spaces may reveal a beauty of their own and are not in need of embellishment. Decorative additions were kitsch and therefore condemnable. Displays of status and wealth, so important in the nineteenth century, were rejected. Symbolic form became superfluous: 'let materials and plants speak for themselves'; spaces were not necessarily determined by surrounding walls but would flow freely between freestanding objects. Straight lines gave strong statements, especially in parallel patterns, but symmetry and axiality were out. Simplicity and clarity in design were called for and details were studied carefully. Functionalism was in vogue and told us to show objects as they are and not to cover them up. While the origins of the aesthetic ideals go back to the Bauhaus era of the 1920s, in post-war years landscape architects looked to the Scandinavian countries, especially Denmark, for sources of inspiration.

Some of these ideals are still discernible or even dominant in contemporary design, as demonstrated in the three LAE books, with the straight lines and crisp details in *Maselake Park* in Berlin (*On Site*), the orderly patterns in *Open spaces in the Spreebogen government district in Berlin* (*Fieldwork*) and the tranquil simplicity of *Weiach churchyard* (*Fieldwork*). At the same time the modernists' abhorrence of embellishment no longer prevails. The decorative patterns in the *Courtyard in Classengade* in Copenhagen, *Garden on Castle Square*, and *Enclosed Garden* enliven visitors' experiences (*In Touch*).

Modernism also represented a political ideology: society could be controlled and the organization of the physical environment was determined via 'top-down' planning rules. Planners and designers created a new, healthy and beautiful environment for the people, provided that they behaved according to rules that were laid down from above. This dogma has proved to be fallacious and today a search continues for opportunities for more private initiative and participation. The involvement of local people in the redesign of *Normand Park* in London (*In Touch*) and the layout of the *Landscape Strip* in Dessau (*On Site*) may be a modest beginning.

A NEED FOR SCIENTIFIC ANALYSIS – THE 1960S. During the 1960s new developments resulted in new challenges: the profession was confronted with more complex assignments at different levels of scale, such as the restructuring of rural landscapes and urban areas. From now on landscape design began to cover all scales of operation and became intertwined with landscape planning, a development which has continued to gain momentum in the 21st century, as seen in *Holland's Green Heart* (*Fieldwork*) and the *Drentse Aa stream landscape* (*On Site*). The *Hub Farms* project also belongs to this category (*In Touch*). Urban park systems became part of the overall urban structure and the inside and outside of urban agglomerations were discernible, as for example in the city of *Bordeaux* (*On Site*). Precise definitions became important and a shared professional language had to be developed (de Jonge 2009, Vroom 2006). The skills of the older generation of garden and landscape architects, based on art and craft, were no longer considered adequate for tackling these tasks, both in urban and rural areas.

In 1960, when I joined the staff of the Parks Division of the Department of Public Works in Amsterdam, I was surprised to see that the existing staff of garden architects was allowed few opportunities to work on the development of urban outdoor space. Town planners and civil engineers dominated the scene and the Parks Department was expected to restrict its activities mostly to drawing up planting plans, with an occasional design assignment for a small park. In rural areas landscape architects were facing similar problems. In reaction to this frustrating experience, the decision was taken to institute landscape architecture as an academic discipline at an increasing number of universities in Europe and elsewhere. The idea behind this was that it would provide landscape architecture professionals with the knowledge and capacity to work together with their counterparts in the planning process on an equal footing.

In the USA Ian McHarg produced his influential book *Design with Nature* in 1969, putting ecological design and planning firmly on the map. Landscape design from now on would be based on a thorough knowledge of physical and biotic factors as well as specifically stated objectives and goals and their consequences. Theory and method became indispensible and landscape analysis became an important instrument. Making use of vertical layers and horizontal patterns, of slopes, drainage systems and soil conditions in order to insert new development into the existing became a compelling need and has remained so up to the present, as illustrated in *Isasco garden estate* (*On Site*) and *Cap Roig* (*Fieldwork*). In other projects historic and natural values have been inserted in a new development or conserved in a creative way, as in the *Strubben Kniphorstbosch* (*In Touch*) with its careful treatment of archaeological sites. At the same time, strong forms, new structures or frameworks have been employed to create stability and new coherence in a complex and changing environment in which new circulation patterns need to be inserted, as in the *Allianz Arena* in Munich (*On Site*) and *De Nieuwe Ooster Cemetery*. (*Fieldwork*).

This design approach leant heavily on new insights based on research in the social and natural sciences and, as a result, the question about the relation between art and science in landscape architecture became urgent. The search for more answers to questions related to human well-being in relation to environmental quality focused on publications by scholars of different disciplines. These began to appear in numbers in the 1960s and 1970s, especially in the United States. The great masters in design history were no longer the only source of information and inspiration, but books and articles by authors like Lynch, Yi Fu Tuan, Rapoport, Alexander, Gehl, Gould, Hall, Hesselgren and many others promised new insights and – for a while – new certainties.

In later years, with the establishment of landscape research institutes during the 1980s – which were dominated by geographers, ecologists and soil scientists – the exact sciences began to wield their influence and helped create a great deal of confusion. Attempts were made to measure the immeasurable and produce certainties where they did not exist. Landscape was viewed as an object to be dissected and analyzed, and was thereby separated from the living landscape which provides a meaningful environment for people. Criteria for quality of a site were specified, rationalized. Sometimes this helped clarify aspects of environmental quality, for instance by defining determinant factors such as vitality, sense, fit, access, control, efficiency and cost. On the whole, however, there was an enormous gap between the paradigms of scientists and the artistic side of landscape architecture and this gap remains today. There is an evident relationship with the scale of operations: the larger the project, the more research based.

In the projects selected by the LAE jury, many examples of site design present creative form with exuberant metaphors and sometimes mystical qualities, such as the *Pedra Tosca Park* and *the Pine Cone Garden* (*On Site*) and sensory delight as encountered in *The City Dune* (*In Touch*). Regional projects on the contrary rely more on extensive research and interdisciplinary cooperation in planning teams, as in the case of *reCreated Nature* (*On Site*). New developments in research methods show that the paradigms of exact sciences are no longer dominant. Design in landscape architecture is often studied with the use of historical methods, for example in garden history, or comparative methods such as in case studies, and empirical methods as used in the natural and social sciences. We learn to distinguish between research in, for, and by design (Lenzholzer 2010).

The reader will not find presentations and expanded discussions on project-related or general research activities in the first two LAE books. The text is mostly limited to the description and evaluation of designs. In this book, *In Touch*, a change can be discerned: a number of projects have been selected for further analysis.

RELEASE FROM PREVIOUS FIGURES – THE 1970S. During the 1970s calls for more democracy and public participation in planning and design demanded new and open planning procedures that would allow for public discussion and choice. Scenarios and design models became part of the design and planning process. In the meantime modernism as a design style in architecture, which started in the midst of such optimism, lost its appeal because of the many examples of monotonous architecture and urban design. Town planners in the Netherlands and elsewhere started to design new neighbourhoods in irregular and curvilinear 'organic' patterns. In 1977 Charles Jencks published his book on postmodern architecture. From now on eclectic form, with an abundance of symbols and metaphors, became the vogue in park design. A striking example is found in Berlin where the site of the former Gestapo seat was converted into *The Topography of Terror* (*On Site*).

Changes in design style in landscape architecture however were not as drastic as in architecture and urban design. Perhaps the materials used and the connection with natural process saved landscape architecture from all too wild variations... One famous exception is Charles Jencks' own Portrack Park in Scotland, which contains an impressive collection of often-mysterious metaphors (Jencks 2003). At the same time in France a younger generation of landscape architects began to produce a new aesthetics in park design with various references to French land-

Modernist ideals: straight lines and orderly patterns in the Spreebogen government district and Maselake Park in Berlin.

Tranquil simplicity in Weiach churchyard.

Embellishment no longer spurned: garden on Castle Square in Lausanne.

Involvement of local people, Normand Park in London.

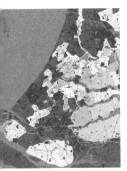

Landscape design across all scales and meshed with planning: Holland's Green Heart, Drentse Aa stream landscape, Hub farms in Twente.

The importance of urban structures: Bordeaux's Miroir d'Eau and Open spaces for the new tramway.

Conservation in a creative way: Strubben Kniphorstbos in Drenthe.

Starting from the existing landscape: Cap Roig in L'Ampolla and Isasco garden estate in Finale Liguria.

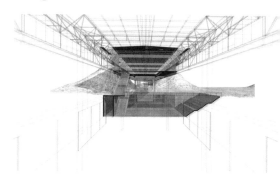

The eclectic form of post modernism in the The Topography of Terror in Berlin.

Strong forms and new structures: creation of a new coherence in Amsterdam's Nieuwe Ooster Cemetery and ...

... in the surroundings of the Allianz Arena in Munich.

...berant metaphors and mystical qualities in the Pine Cone Garden in Padula...

...and in Pedra Tosca Park in Les Preses and The City Dune in Copenhagen.

...w aesthetics in park design in the Landschaftspark Riem in Munich and Les Jardins d'Éole in Paris.

Professional design for the exterior spaces of housing projects: Funenpark in Amsterdam and Waterrijk in Eindhoven.

Designing infrastructure and urban development plans: Glattal railway in Zurich and Les Horts de Villabertran in Figueres.

Sensitive projects founded on comprehensive research: recreated Nature in the Scheldt estuary...

... and the Scheldt Quays.

Design exploring new uses and transitory forms: the haphazard laissez-faire of Essen's Zollverein Park.

scapes, combined with a free choice of symbolic objects and elegant combinations of materials, as in *Les Jardins d'Éole* in Paris (*On Site*). At the same time, the modernist preference for long and powerful straight lines and distant views between orderly patterns was still in evidence, as in *Landschaftspark Riem* in Munich (*Fieldwork*).

MULTIPLE MODES ON THE HORIZON – THE 1980S. From the 1980s until the present day a trend towards diversification both in design styles and in design assignments has continued and it has become difficult to distinguish a dominant movement and a well-defined task. Gone was the time when town planners and engineers put landscape architects in their 'proper place', regarding them as mere tree planters. At present their professional competence covers all aspects of outdoor space housing projects, as in *Funen Park* in Amsterdam (*In Touch*) and *Waterrijk* in Eindhoven (*On Site*), or infrastructural and urban planning works like *Els Horts de Vilabertran* in Catalonia and *Glattalbahn* in Zurich (*In Touch*).

TWO REMAINING QUESTIONS. At the start of the LAE project in 2002 the founders were hoping they would find some common denominator in the entries, which would show that something like a European heritage actually exists. After going through the collection of projects in the three books, my overall conclusion is that in terms of form and pattern individual approaches proliferate, while at the same time the heritage from the past is still discernible from the way each site is assessed in terms of context, history, natural strata. There are common values indeed. In the meantime two main themes continue to dominate discussions on the way landscape architects should operate and how they should view the world. There still are conflicts which have not been solved. One is the schism between the need for a rational and systematic approach to complex assignments versus the traditional art of designing. The other is found in the different stands on the issue of the moral aspects of interventions in natural systems. These questions have been raised and discussed in a number of projects and essays contained in the LAE books, but further in-depth investigation is needed.

HOW CAN LANDSCAPE ANALYSIS AND DESIGN BE COMBINED? Landscape and site analysis have proved to be an important tool for supporting and guiding the design process, especially for regional projects that must rely on a thorough knowledge of environmental factors. The analytic approach helps organize a design assignment in its initial phase. Gone is the time when an inexperienced student desperately sits facing a white sheet of paper, not knowing how to tackle his or her assignment. From now on he/she is helped on his way by applying knowledge in a systematic way via logical reasoning (Hauxner 2009). Such a rational approach tends to reduce the complexity of an assignment; uncertainties are removed by applying rational models. In general we see that the practice of landscape architecture, especially at the higher scales, is no longer an arts-and-craft approach but a combination of creative thinking, systematic procedures and applied scientific knowledge (de Jonge 2009).

In the meantime fellow disciplines in academia regard a newcomer like landscape architecture as a stranger in their midst, and in order to remain an accepted colleague it must constantly try and prove its scientific aspirations, not only in the way the design process is organized but also in terms of published research reports, and this puts enormous pressure on the discipline. But how scientific can landscape architecture be? We can claim some analogy between scientific research method and landscape analysis, as both begin with an inventory of available data.

There is a reduction process in the sense that only those data that are relevant for the design are selected. The relevance is established by checking the data against design goals and objectives. A design is structured on the basis of design principles, goals and objectives that help digest the collected information and prepare for the actual design phase. Like scientists, the designers have their paradigms even if they do not seem to be aware of this all the time. Take the following (translated) excerpt from an interview with Dutch town planner Ben Eerhart in 1984. It opened with the question: 'How are landscape architects faring?' The answer was: 'Contemporary dynamics make them nervous, the eternal cliché 'when the tree is mature, the planter is dead' keeps pursuing them. The time when they were always called in too late in a project to make amendments is fresh in their memories, and recent emancipation is still fragile, in as far as it is achieved at all. They therefore apply 'strong forms', rectilinear or curved, or base lines that can withstand changes over time and survive, just like the great 17th century estates survived. The notion of form should not be taken too narrowly, because it may also mean exerting a strong grasp, as a meagre interpretation of the notion of 'concept'.'

Landscape analysis may be a useful and even an indispensible tool, but the problem is that, on its own, it will not result in a satisfactory plan. Landscape is more than a combination of biotic, abiotic and land-use factors. It means scenery, a setting or a stage for action, old and new stories, dialect and culture. Designing is more than distributing types of land use, like the solving of a jigsaw puzzle of which the parts must closely fit together. Design is also an artistic activity, creating three-dimensional compositions, playing with objects and spaces and people, with imagination and sensory delight. How can we combine these demands?

An answer is given in a statement by Michael van Gessel, who trained as a landscape architect in Wageningen: 'In the functionalist approach, a functional design seems to grow by itself as a product of a clear confrontation between an analysis of the landscape and an analysis of the programme of requirements. That is our school, our history. But that sometimes results in highly predictable, or even boring designs. Where it is possible to uncouple the form from content for a moment, it is possible to arrive at other forms, because, for a moment, you are entirely free.' (Steenhuis 2011) In Van Gessel's opinion the existing landscape should never be regarded as a straightjacket but as a structure that can be adapted. This means creating conditions for future development. There is a need for clear and understandable designs and this is connected with a constant search for the essence. A search by means of sketches should lead to designs consisting of simple spaces that are tied together by a limited number of lines. Such structures are normally flexible. 'Some restraint in the equipment of simple open spaces is called for. Space is all we need and nothing else.' (Steenhuis ibid)

In the first two LAE books, examples of extensive landscape and site analysis are not much in evidence. The size of the books and the need to condense presentations in a few pages make extended surveys difficult to include. However for a keen observer there is more than meets the eye. It is evident that for instance the *Scheldt Quays* and the *Recreated Nature* projects (*On Site*) are founded on a type of extensive study which deserves more attention in future publications.

A CALL FROM NATURE? Throughout history landscape architects have been occupied with the relation between man and nature and have attempted in their designs to symbolize this relationship, as is visible in historic design styles. However, during the late 1960s their efforts came under attack with the arrival of the discipline of landscape ecology, a field of science focusing on the relation between abiotic and biotic factors at the regional level. The concept of nature changed from an environment in which man acts as its steward, to a nature that is by definition not touched by human hands, and is not to be touched. Biology claimed to be the provider of moral guidelines for all interventions in the environment. The architectural concepts of landscape architects were distrusted, the prime goal of ecologists being maximum ecological diversity, no matter in what form (Vroom 1997). In this view all landscape changes result in decay, unless implemented for the purpose of the creating new eco-types. In the project for Reykjavik's Art Museum (*In Touch*) Martha Schwarz sarcastically puts it this way: 'In the USA, landscape and nature are understood to be the same thing. As a result, it is a given that any built landscape has a moral imperative to represent nature (as long as the trees don't get in the way of viewing the building).' Anne Whiston Spirn comments that '(...) every garden is a product of natural phenomena and human artifice. It is impossible to make a garden without expressing, however unconsciously, ideas about nature (...)'. However, 'designers who refer to their work as 'natural' or 'ecological' make ideas of nature central and explicit, citing nature as authority to justify decisions (...)'. Spirn advises caution: 'Appealing to nature as the authority for landscape design has pitfalls which are often overlooked by advocates of 'natural' gardens (...). Some (...) have embraced ecology as the *primary* authority for determining the 'natural' (and therefore correct) way to design landscapes. (...) Given the many meanings and contested definitions of what is natural, appeal to nature as authority for human actions is problematic (...). The emphasis should be on a spirit of inquiry and exploration rather than close-minded certainty.' (Spirn 1997)

Luckily there are excellent examples of projects that inquire, explore and show how to deal with the relation between human artefact and natural process in a sensitive and creative way. Outstanding schemes are the *Cap de Creus Project* in Cadaqués (*In Touch*), the seemingly haphazard *laissez-faire Zollverein Park* (*On Site*) and the *Strubben Kniphorstbosch* (*In Touch*), as well as many others which show that landscape architects can come to grips with such complex issues, provided they are given the means.

References
[1] M. Hauxner, *Drawing & Reading: Integration of academic and artistic work/ Made or Given: Form and information in the art of cultivation*, 2009.
[2] M. Hauxner, *Fra Naturlig Natur till Supernatur*, 2010.
[3] C. Jencks, *The Language of Post-Modern Architecture*, 1977.
[4] C. Jencks, *The Garden of Cosmic speculation*, 2003.
[5] J. de Jonge, *Landscape Architecture between Politics and science*, PhD thesis Wageningen University, 2009.
[6] B. Latour, *A Cautious Prometheus? A few steps towards a philosophy of design*. Keynote lecture, Networks of design meeting, Design History Society Cornwall, 2008.
[7] S. Lenzholzer, *Designing Atmospheres. Research and Design for thermal comfort in Dutch urban squares*, PhD thesis Wageningen University, 2010.
[8] I. McHarg, *Design with Nature*, 1969.
[9] A. Spirn, 'The Authority of Nature. Conflict and Confusion in Landscape Architecture' in Joachim Wolschke Bulmahn (ed), *Nature and Ideology*, 1997.
[10] M. Steenhuis, 2011. *Bureau B&B. Urbanism and Landscape Architecture. Collective Genius 1977-2010*, 2011, pp. 53-57.
[11] M. J. Vroom, 1977 'Images of an ideal landscape and the consequences. The landscape of ecosystems' in G. Thompson & F. Steiner (ed) *Ecological design and planning*, 1977, pp. 301-305.
[12] M. J. Vroom, *Lexicon of Garden and Landscape Architecture*, 2006.

Meto J. Vroom is professor emeritus of the Chair of Landscape Architecture at Wageningen University, the Netherlands, and chairman of the Landscape Architecture Europe Foundation (LAE).

EDITED BY
Landscape Architecture Europe Foundation (LAE)
Schip van Blaauw, Generaal Foulkesweg 72
6703 BW Wageningen
The Netherlands
www.landscapearchitectureeurope.com

BOARD OF THE FOUNDATION
Meto J. Vroom *(chairman, professor emeritus of landscape architecture at Wageningen University)*
Kathryn Moore *(professor of landscape architecture at Birmingham City University)*
Alastair McCapra *(treasurer, chief executive at the Landscape Institute, London)*
Fritz Auweck, Munich *(past president of the European Federation for Landscape Architecture (EFLA), Munich)*
Maria Goula *(vice dean of landscape studies at the School of Architecture of Barcelona (UPC))*

SELECTION JURY
Michael van Gessel *(chairman, landscape architect, Amsterdam)*
Tone Lindheim *(landscape architect, director of Bjørbekk & Lindheim AS, Oslo)*
Lilli Lička *(landscape architect, partner of koselicka landscape architecture, Vienna)*
Antonio Angelillo *(architect, director of ACMA, co-director of UPC's master in landscape architecture, Milan)*
João Nunes Ferreira *(landscape architect, director of PROAP landscape architecture, Lisbon)*

EDITORIAL BOARD
Lisa Diedrich *(chief editor, professor of landscape architecture at SLU Alnarp, researcher and editor, Munich)*
Mark Hendriks *(spatial planner, journalist, editor of Blauwe Kamer, Utrecht)*
Claudia Moll *(landscape architect, researcher, editor, Zurich)*
Thierry Kandjee *(landscape architect, partner of TAKTYK, researcher, Brussels)*
Alice Labadini *(guest editor, architect, researcher at Oslo Architecture School, Oslo)*

ADMINISTRATION AND PRODUCTION
Harry Harsema *(producer, landscape architect and publisher, Wageningen)*
Mark Hendriks *(desk editor)*
Annemarie Roetgerink *(secretary Landscape Architecture Europe Foundation (LAE) Wageningen)*

ESSAYS
Steven Delva, Lisa Diedrich, Maria Goula, Maria Hellström, Ana Kučan, Mads Farsø, Eric Luiten, Claudia Moll, Svava Riesto, Martin Søberg and Ellen Braae, Ingrid Sarlöv Herlin, Hille von Seggern, Meto J. Vroom, Anna Zahonero

PROJECT FEATURES AND ICONS
Lisa Diedrich (ld)
Mark Hendriks (mh)
Claudia Moll (cl)
Thierry Kandjee (tk)
Alice Labadini

ENGLISH TRANSLATION
Carmen Grau (French-English, German-English)
Marion Frandsen (Danish-English)
Sara van Otterloo-Butler (Dutch-English)
Laurie Neale (Dutch-English)
Julian Reisenberger (German-English)
Diane Schaap (German-English)
Almuth Seebohm (German-English)

COPY EDITING
Sara van Otterloo-Butler

DESIGN
Daphne de Bruijn and Harry Harsema, Blauwdruk Publishers
with Janna and Hilde Meeus, Amsterdam

LITHOGRAPHY AND IMAGE PROCESSING
Wim van Hof, GAW design and communication, Wageningen

ILLUSTRATIONS
The map of Europe and the location maps were drawn by Thierry Kandjee, TAKTYK
The photos of the jury and editors were taken by Hans Dijkstra and Harry Harsema
All other illustrations are by the authors and the selected offices, unless noted otherwise

PRINTING
Lecturis, Eindhoven, The Netherlands
Printed on acid-free paper produced from chlorine free pulp. TCF ∞

IP catalogue record for this book is available
n the Library of Congress, Washington D.C.,
A.

iographic information published by the
man National Library
German National Library lists this publication
he Deutsche Nationalbibliografie; detailed
iographic data are available on the Internet at
://dnb.d-nb.de.

2012 Birkhäuser, Basel
. Box, CH-4002 Basel, Switzerland
t of De Gruyter
N 978-3-0346-0815-2

ldwide distribution except the Netherlands by
khäuser
w.birkhauser.com

2012 Landscape Architecture Europe
undation, Wageningen
d Blauwdruk Publishers
neraal Foulkesweg 72, 6703 BW Wageningen,
Netherlands
N 978-90-75271-80-5

stribution for participants in the LAE project
d members of the European Federation for
ndscape Architecture (EFLA) and the European
uncil of Landscape Architecture School (ECLAS)
the LAE Foundation
w.landscapearchitectureeurope.com

stribution in the Netherlands by Blauwdruk
blishers
w.uitgeverijblauwdruk.nl

Landscape Architecture Europe is an initiative of
the Landscape Architecture Europe Foundation
(LAE) and the European Federation for Landscape
Architecture (EFLA) within the International
Federation of Landscape Architects (IFLA).

PREVIOUS PUBLICATIONS OF LANDSCAPE
ARCHITECTURE EUROPE
FIELDWORK (2006) is available in an English and
a German language edition (Birkhäuser), a Dutch
language edition (Thoth Publishers) and a French
language edition (Infolio)
ON SITE (2009) is available in an English and a
German language edition (Birkhäuser), a Dutch
language edition (Blauwdruk), a French language
edition (Actes Sud) and a Spanish language edition (Gustavo Gili).

SPONSORS

The publication was made possible by the
financial support from
EFLA European Federation for Landscape
Architecture
IFLA International Federation of Landscape
Architects
NH BOSstichting
The Netherlands Architecture Fund

SPONSORS
Adviesbureau Haver Droeze BNT
Ambius Nederland
Ank Bleeker en Anneke Nauta
landschapsarchitecten BNT
Asplan Viak AS
Bjørbekk & Lindheim Landskapsarkitekter
Boomkwekerij Ebben
Bruns Pflanzen
BSLA Bund Schweizer Landschaftsarchitekten
Bugel Hajema Adviseurs Ruimtelijke ordening
en Milieu
Bureau B + B stedenbouw en
landschapsarchitectuur
Buro Lubbers landschapsarchitectuur
& stedelijk ontwerp
Buro Mien Ruys tuin & landschapsarchitekten
Buro Sant en Co Landschapsarchitectuur
Buro Schokland landschap, ontwerp en verhaal
Citec civiel en cultuurtechnisch adviesburo
Copijn Tuin- en Landschapsarchitecten
Croonen Adviseurs ruimtelijke vormgeving
& ordening
DS landschapsarchitecten
Elings vormgevers van natuur en landschap
Feddes Olthof landschapsarchitecten
Feste Grenland AS
Grindaker AS Landskapsarkitekter
Grontmij N.V.
H+N+S Landschapsarchitecten

Hollandschap Adviesburo voor Stad-
en Landschapsinrichting
Hosper landschapsarchitectuur en stedebouw
IAA architecten
ir. Ben Kuipers landschapsarchitect
John van Veelen landschapsarchitect
Karres en Brands landschapsarchitecten
Katie Tedder landschapsarchitect
Koninklijke Ginkel Groep
Kuiper Compagnons
Landlab studio voor landschapsarchitectuur
Landskapsfabrikken
Lodewijk Wiegersma
Loos van Vliet atelier voor stedenbouw, landsch
architectuur
M.J. De Nijs en Zonen BV Bouwbedrijf
Projectontwikkeling
Mathieu Derckx Stedenbouw
Landschapsarchitectuur
Mostert De Winter BV
NXT landscapes office for landscape architectur
urban design & regional planning
OKRA landschapsarchitecten
Quadrat atelier voor stedebouw, landschap en
architectuur
Rijnboutt Architectuur
Robbert De Koning landschapsarchitect BNT
Rod'or advies
Rotzler Krebs Partner Landschaftsarchitekten
Schønherr A/S
Smedsvig Landskapsarkitekter AS
SmitsRinsma
Strootman Landschapsarchitecten
Van den Berk Boomkwekerijen
Van der Tol BV
Van Empelen Van Aalderen Partners BV
landschapsarchitecten
Van Hees tuin- en landschapsarchitectuur
Veenenbos en Bosch landschapsarchitecten
Vestre AS
VlugP stedebouw & landschapsarchitectuur
Vollmer & Partners stedebouw en landschap
VS landschapsarchitectuur
West 8 Urban Design & Landscape Architecture